AGAINST FALSE UNION

SAINT PHOTIOS
Patriarch of Constantinople
(who is commemorated on the sixth of February)

He who was worthily called Great, was a most wise and great confessor, having struggled courageously against the various heretics — Iconoclasts, Manicheans, and the Latin-minded. He, the blessed one, being hated by the Papists, underwent many hardships and persecutions for the Orthodox Faith, according to the Word of the Lord: "If they have hated Me, they will hate you also." All the Orthodox pray and seek his intercession, chanting unto his memory:

As one like unto the Apostles
And a teacher of the ecumene,
Beseech the Master of all
That He may grant peace to the ecumene
And to our souls the great mercy.

SAINT MARK EVGENIKOS OF EPHESUS

The great champion of the Orthodox Faith, Metropolitan of Ephesus. At the accursed synod in Ferrara and Florence he was the dauntless soldier of Christ, warring against both the deceitful Latins and his Pope-worshipping compatriots. Because of his laborious struggles for Orthodoxy he received the un-withering crown from the prize-bestowing Christ; and the race of Orthodox Greeks, which was saved from destruction, owes him eternal gratitude. He is commemorated on the nineteenth day of January.

The Foundation of those that hope on Thee, O Lord, make steadfast the Church which Thou hast purchased with Thine own precious Blood.

Alexander Kalomiros

AGAINST FALSE UNION

Humble thoughts of an Orthodox Christian
concerning the attempts for union of the One,
Holy, Catholic, and Apostolic Church with
the so-called Churches of the West.

With a Prologue by

Photios Kontoglou

Translated from the Greek by

George Gabriel

Published by
St. Nectarios Press
Seattle, Washington

ISBN Number 0-913026-49-2

Printed in the United States of America

TABLE OF CONTENTS

CHAPTER THREE

REVISED APPENDIX

PREFACE

From the time of its first appearance in 1967, Alexander Kalomiros' *Against False Union* has been widely acclaimed. Orthodox and non-Orthodox alike have made reference to it, quoting especially from its chapters on ecclesiology, salvation, and the participation of the Orthodox Catholic Church in the "World Council of Churches." We now offer a fourth printing of this timely and enlightening publication with a revised Appendix.

In these days, when "because of the abounding of iniquity the love of many hath grown cold," we pray that this book will continue to be a source of inspiration, edification, and guidance unto salvation for pious and Orthodox Christians, as well as for those who are not of the Orthodox Faith. Amen. So be it.

SAINT NECTARIOS AMERICAN ORTHODOX CHURCH

2000

PREFACE TO FIRST EDITION

Let them bring forth their witnesses, and be justified, and let them hear, and declare the 'truth. Be ye my witnesses, and I also am witness, saith the Lord God, and My servant whom I have chosen: that ye may know, and believe, and understand that I am He.

Esaias 43:9-10

In the Name of the Father and Son and Holy Spirit. Amen.

It is with spiritual joy and gladdening of heart that we offer this, our first English publication in book form, to the pious Orthodox Christians for study and edification. It is a short but timely little book in these troubled days of apostasy and unbelief. It first appeared in Greek (1963), published by "Astir," and was acclaimed for its clarity and sincerity wherever it was read. The fathers of the Holy Mountain consider it God-inspired and recommend it highly. The chapters on ecclesiology and eschatology are unparalleled.

Praise and glory be to our good God that He hath raised up among His people zealous young men to defend our Holy Orthodox Faith! The author is a pious physician, married and with children, who is living in Northern Greece, Dr. Alexander Kalomiros. The translation was done by another pious layman (with a theological degree), also married, living in New York City, George Gabriel. The expense of the present publication was covered by a second pious physician, also married and with children, Dr. Efstathios Metropoulos of Detroit, Michigan. To all the above we are indebted.

We have thought it wise at the end to append four short items related to the subject of the book. The first is an article, "Is the Papacy a Church?" by the same author, which sets forth the Orthodox viewpoint, based on the Canons and the Holy Fathers, concerning the existence or non-existence of Holy Mysteries (Sacraments) outside the Church. The second item is a proclamation of the fathers of the Holy Mountain concerning the uniate tendencies of the Patriarchate of Constantinople. The third is a magnificent letter of protest by the Most Reverend Metropolitan Philaret, First Hierarch of the Russian Orthodox Church Outside of Russia, concerning the lifting of the Anathemas of 1054 by Patriarch Athenagoras. And the fourth is an open letter to the same Patriarch by "The Three Hierarchs."

We are sure that for serious-minded Orthodox Christians the present little volume will offer much food for study and thought.

Asking for your holy prayers, we remain: the Editors and Publishers,

Holy Transfiguration Monastery
Boston, Massachusetts

PROLOGUE

For neither at any time have we used flattering words,
as ye know, nor a cloak of covetousness; God is witness,
nor of men sought we glory.

(I Thess. 2:5)

It is possible to find a middle word that between two
views will signify both. But a middle view between two
opposite views concerning the same thing is impossible....
There is no room for compromise in matters of the
Orthodox Faith.

(St. Mark of Ephesus)

Truly "great is the mystery of piety," as the blessed Apostle Paul says. Piety and faith, because they are mysteries, yield fruits that knowledge cannot give.

The author of this book is not a theologian trained in the schools where they study the unstudiable — theology. He studied medicine, something which can be studied because it is worldly, human knowledge. He drew his Orthodox Faith and piety from Tradition. He received it in the way, as he himself says, faith and piety are transmitted — from teacher to disciple, from parent to child, from elder to disciple, from Christian to Christian. For this reason he "is one who experiences divine things, not one who learns about them," having faith as a guide and not knowledge. "He walks by faith and not by sight," as the Apostle Paul says. And this is why his book is harsh; it does not have the compromises that reveal little faith, nor accomodations to avoid unpleasantness for people of contrary views, nor any false brotherliness. Devotion to truth permits no concessions. His book is harsh and brusque, although the author himself is in fact humble, peaceable, meek, gracious, and modest. But faith gives him the sword of the Spirit, and this humble, sensible, and gracious man, filled with love, appears harsh and brusque. Does not St. John the Theologian, the preacher of love, seem to be harsher and brusquer than the other Apostles and preachers of the Gospel, as he appears in his First Epistle and in the Book of Revelation?

The author of this book is young. But "let no one disdain his youth." I made his spiritual acquaintance when he was studying medicine in Switzerland, and we were publishing the periodical **Kibotos** (the *Ark*). He wrote me a letter then about some satanic articles by a Roman Catholic in the newspaper *Le Courrier,* and asked us to protect our Orthodox Faith from the snares of heretics. Afterwards, he wrote me many letters, and to the present day he writes me letters which are always very informative and beneficial, and which have the sweet fragrance of deep faith and love for our holy Tradition. This is why I insistently urged him to write at greater length on the subjects he briefly outlined in his letters. And I asked him to consent to their being printed in a book, knowing his modesty. Finally he consented, and this small book is the first which he has sent to the publisher, Mr. Alexander Papademetriou, who offered with pleasure to publish it.

We realize this book, written "with much understanding," will be condemned by many people as rude and bad-tempered, for in our hypocritical time only those men are respected as genuine Christians who do not have within their hearts the fire of faith, and especially of the Orthodox (that is, the true) Faith—and this is why they are lukewarm, spiritless, compromising, and obliging, as are many of those persons systematically involved in theology. The world has learned to regard such people as good and forbearing Christians, whereas it detests those who are like the author of this book—that is, "fervid in spirit"—as fanatics, intolerant, superstitious, and narrow-minded worshippers of empty forms. Alas! today theologians have ended up being "disputers of this world." Men who are concerned with religion write piles of books, big and important, filled with so-called "theological learning" which, owing to its method of inquiry into religious matters, is nothing else than the worldly knowledge the Apostle Paul calls "vain deceit" and "cunning deception." The Holy Gospel, which is simplicity itself, is dissected, examined, and dismembered according to systems of philosophy, of "vain deceit." Confusion, complexity, theories which confuse man, "foolish searchings and geneologies and legalistic battles," mud which clouds the clear water springing up unto eternal life, all these things are written in the name of Him Who came into the world to save the lost sheep — the man of vain knowledge — from the burden of his sinful mind, crying: "Come unto Me all ye who are heavy laden with foolish and purposeless wisdom." Piles of papers are written in the name of Christ and His Gospel, which the simplest heart experiences; while those who write these innumerable books have been wandering around in the maze and the darkness of their own wisdom, far from the Christ they have forgotten, engulfed by the vanities of their own intellects. Their hearts no longer feel the breath of God; they are deadened and dried up by their self-conceited wisdom for which men honor them.

The divine-tongued Apostle Paul meant them when he wrote, "For the time will come when they will not endure sound doctrine: but after their own desires shall they heap to themselves teachers, tickling their hearing; and they shall turn away their ears from the truth and shall be turned unto fables" (II Tim. 4:3,4). "They shall heap to themselves teachers" — they shall bring forth many teachers, and in hearing them they shall be gratified because their empty wisdom shall tickle their ears. But in order that they may not hear the truth, the simple truth of religion, they shall stop up their ears while they wish to be told myths, that is, theories and fantasies void of meaning. Thus today do we not see such "heaps" of teachers who with their talk tickle the ears of students and other Christians?

And so Kalomiros' book will upset those spirits who have reduced the religion of Christ to a system of worldly knowledge, to rationalism, who detest and mock every "sound doctrine," which for them is a naive conception of religion, filled with the superstitions of tradition. In fact, what can anything written by a man like Kalomiros who has not been to a big school (especially a foreign one) be to them?

But fortunate Kalomiros drank from the spring of the living

water, from Tradition, and studied the Fathers day and night. And having faith as his guide he was "taught by God." Christ says, "When the good shepherd putteth forth his own sheep, he goeth forth before them, and the sheep follow him for they know his voice" (John 10:4). That is, "My disciples hear My words with a simple spirit, and they accept them in their hearts without passing them through their complicated intellects and creating theories; they accept them with faith like the innocent sheep which hear the voice of the shepherd and run close to him." Faith opens the mouth of the believer, and His preaching opens the hearts of Christians, according to the saying of Christ Who said: "He that believeth on Me, as the Scripture hath said, out of his belly shall flow rivers of living water" (John 7:38).

Those of "foolish wisdom" who teach "in persuasive words of human wisdom" do not accept the true preachers of the Gospel, and this is because the true preachers do not conform to this world, but are "transformed by the renewal of their mind" (Rom. 12:2).

They will find, therefore, many occasions in this book for condemnation. They will condemn the author for not having the hypocritical affability they have towards heretics, in spite of the fact that the author is not impertinent, but has the courage of a soldier of Christ and proceeds according to the words of the Apostle Paul, who said: "For God hath not given us the spirit of fear, but of power and of love and of wisdom" (II Tim. 1:7).

Another fault they will find is that his message is watered with affliction in Christ, with gladdening sorrow; whereas they are optimistic, having their minds turned to the things of this world. But let them see what the Apostle Paul says: "Sorrow in God worketh repentance to salvation not to be repented of, but the sorrow of the world worketh death" (II Cor. 7:10). The sorrow a man who believes in God goes through is sorrow which is sweetened by hope, and this is why it is a joyful sorrow, "gladdening sorrow," and with repentance it brings him to the salvation of his soul.

I praise this blessed young man* who has written such an edifying book — one that breathes forth the spirit of true Orthodoxy. And I glorify and laud the all-honorable name of the Lord, Who gives to the Orthodox Church jewels such as these, which shine in the darkness of error and ruin. May our very merciful Lord and God be glorified and blessed, Who makes steadfast the Orthodox Faith with such stones that "the builders reject."

Photios Kontoglou

* I beg the reader to permit me to add a few lines here which I think should be read from a letter which Mr. Kalomiros sent me.

"I thank you very much for your kind words. They are an encouragement for me, which I need very much. Here where I live, I do not know anyone who thinks this way and who understands me. I do not have discussions with atheists and the indifferent. And then again, the pious look upon me with distrust and suspicion. Only when I read the Fathers and lives of the Saints do I find consolation. Sometimes I fear that perhaps I am in error. Whatever I regard as important, everyone else regards as trivial; and again whatever I consider trivial, everyone else, both the pious and the atheists, consider important.

"Moreover, I thank you for cautioning me about arrogance. This is how I know that you are a true friend. Pray that I do not fall into arrogance. At any rate I must be very stupid if something like that happens to me. I see very clearly that all that I write I have borrowed from the Fathers. Nothing is my own. That is why I defend them with so much fanaticism. Yesterday I was telling my wife that many people have no idea about the things I write, and yet they are living them. And I know all these things, but I do not live them. That is why many times as I was writing, I felt that I should quit, but I continued writing, because that way, at least, I was able to gather my thoughts upon God, even if my heart remained frozen.

With the love of Christ,
Alexander"

CHAPTER ONE

I. PEACE WITHOUT TRUTH

The tragic experience of recent generations has brought to humanity an intense thirst for peace. Peace is now considered a good higher than many ideals for which people formerly gladly shed their blood. Contributing very much to this is the fact that war is not what it often was in the past, that is, a conflict between injustice and justice, but has become a conflict without meaning between injustice and injustice. The experience of falsehood and hypocrisy, which the injustice of various parties has used to appear just in the eyes of its followers, has caused people to lose faith in the existence of justice and to fail to see anything before them that is worthy of defending. Thus war, in any form, seems to be something completely absurd.

This reluctance on the part of humanity for any kind of conflict would have been something admirable if it were the offspring of spiritual health. If injustice, hatred, and falsehood had ceased to exist, then peace would have been the consummation of human happiness. Unity would have been a natural and not an artificial result. But something totally different is noticeable. Today when everyone is speaking of peace and unity, self-love and hatred, injustice and falsehood, ambition and greed, are at their zenith. All — everyone in his own way — speak of love for man, of love for humanity. But there has never existed a greater hypocrisy than that so-called love. Because love towards something theoretical, for something imaginary, such as the concept "humanity," is equally theoretical and imaginary. It has no relation to love for the particular man we have before us. This love for a particular person, when it exists, is the only real love. It is the love for our neighbor that Christ asked.

This particular man with his imperfections and weaknesses, instead of being loved, has been hated in our time more than in any other age. Not only has he been hated, but he has been scorned and humiliated; he has been regarded as a "thing" without any particular value, a means for the attainment of "high goals," a particle of the mass. Those who speak the most of love towards man and humanity, of peace and union, are precisely those who hate their neighbor, their acquaintance, the most. They love man the creation of their own imagination; they do not love man the reality. This worship of the idol "man" is in reality narcissism; it is the worship of the ego.

It would be naivete, therefore, if one were to believe that the pacifist disposition that characterizes humanity today proceeds from love. These words about love are hypocrisy and self-deception. The desire for peace proceeds from the loss of ideals, from fear, and from the love of comfort. It is the desire to be left in peace to enjoy the good things of this earth. It is the conventional cooperation for the acquisition of goods which each person separately would not be able to acquire. It is a universal understanding upon something which has become the passion of the whole earth: sensualism and materialism. It is a product of necessity.

The peace of which the world speaks is an unconditional capitulation of everything good and sacred and great, and the dominance of pettiness, mediocrity, and lukewarmness. It is the blotting out of the personality of individuals and of peoples. It is a marmelade of compromises and calculations, a sea of hypocrisy, indifference for the truth, the betrayal of everything holy and sacred.

War is a terrible thing, a result of the fall of man, and no one is about to praise it. But the peace for which the world is haggling is something infinitely more fearful. A fever is a very unpleasant thing, but it shows at least that the organism is reacting against something bad which has entered it. The peace which they wish to bring is not, unfortunately, that which comes from the victory over evil, but that which comes from defeat. It is the feverlessness of a corpse.

At bottom, the peace which men pursue is not only a peace of weapons. It is the peace of conscience. They wish to reconcile good with evil, justice with injustice, virtue with sin, truth with falsehood, in order to be able to make peace with their conscience.

II. THERE HAS BEEN NO SEVERANCE

So-called Christians play a significant role in the world's effort for peace. With the slogan "Christians unite," they set out for the bazar where truth will be sold out.

Once, Christians had faith and were ready to die for their Faith. Today their zeal for the truth has cooled. They have begun to consider it as something secondary. They find the differences between churches, for which in former times Martyrs eagerly sacrificed themselves, the Fathers were exiled, and the faithful mutilated, as unimportant and unworthy of mention.

Most of them are sickly and incorrigible sentimentalists who think that the religion of Christ is an ethical system concerning human relations. Others pursue political purposes and dark interests. All of them together are building the city of Antichrist. They seek union, being indifferent to truth; they seek an external rapprochement, ignoring internal dissensions; they seek the letter, being indifferent to the spirit.

How is it possible for them to hope that what failed in the first centuries of the schism shall be accomplished now that the differences in dogma and mentality have, with the passage of centuries, widened from breaches to gulfs?

The mere fact that they speak of the union of the churches shows that their thought is quite anti-Christian. They thereby concede that the One, Holy, Catholic, and Apostolic Church which we confess in our Symbol of Faith (Creed) has ceased to exist; that it has been severed into many churches which are no longer catholic, that is, they no longer contain the whole truth and grace as do the local Orthodox churches, but have a greater or lesser part of truth and grace. Consequently, they think that the truth no longer exists upon the earth and that Christ came in vain. For in the confusion of the truth with falsehood, it is impossible for the truth to which Christ came to bear witness to be rediscovered. And hence it is impossible to rediscover Christ, Who is Himself the Truth.

But then why did Christ say that He will be with us until the end of the world? "And I will be with you all the days unto the end of the world." Why did He say that the Holy Spirit will guide the disciples to the fulness of truth and that the gates of Hades will not be able to prevail against the Church?

If the Church has been divided — and if it has need of union, it means it has been divided — then all that Christ has promised has turned out to be lies! But God forbid such blasphemy! The Church lives and will live until the end of the world, undivided and invulnerable, according to the promise of the Lord. All who speak of "union of the churches" simply deny Christ and His Church.

When an Orthodox patriarch accepts the participation of the Orthodox Church in the Protestant World Council of Churches as one among many "churches," what else is he doing but publicly confessing, like the Protestants, the existence of many churches, and therefore the division of the One, Holy, Catholic, and Apostolic Church? What else is he doing but denying Christ?

But in their profane efforts, these people bring forward the Church's liturgical texts and Christ Himself as their allies. Indeed, Christ prayed for His disciples "that they may be one," and the Church prays at every Liturgy "for the union of all (*hyper tes ton panton henoseos*)."*

But these phrases do not mean that the Church prays that someday Christians should be united with mutual compromises in their beliefs. They do not refer to pursuits of compromising agreements by which variously named elements are united. They have no relation to the protocols for an alliance, or agreement, or union, such as those between different nations which are signed after many negotiations. No, these phrases mean none of these things. The

---

* "All" here does not refer to "churches." In Greek *panton* is a masculine adjective and therefore refers to "all the faithful." If the reference were to all "churches," then the proper adjective would have been *pason*, instead of *panton*. The context evidently indicates that "all" refers to all the faithful, since the immediately preceding prayer is for the "good estate of the holy churches of God," i.e., the local, regional Orthodox churches (parishes) wherever they may be, which comprise the One, Holy, Catholic, and Apostolic Church. "Churches" here does not mean, as many wrongly say, the different denominations outside Orthodoxy. It is natural then that there should follow in the same petition a prayer for the union in Christ of all the faithful who comprise the local Orthodox churches. Those outside the Church (the

Church does not pray to God that variously opposed elements be united, but that all men should become ONE. In other words, that they should all accept the truth with great contrition and humbly prostrate before the Church and be numbered among her members. That they come to realize the error under which they have lived and hasten to the light and the truth, that is, to the Church. This is what the Church prays for. Exactly what she also prays for in the Liturgy of St. Basil the Great: "Return [O Lord] those in error and unite them to Thy Catholic and Apostolic Church." Only this prayer and desire proceeds from genuine love, because it seeks the healing of the sick and not their delusion.

III. OFFERING, NOT DISCUSSION

A few naive Orthodox think that this rapprochement of the churches is not taking place for the purpose of union, but for the purpose of enlightenment and mission to the heterodox. "These are," they say, "manifestations of love for our brothers." "If we shut ourselves in our shell," they often say, "if we do not attend the international conferences and send observers to the Papal synods, etc., then how will the Westerners know the Orthodox Church, and how will they be attracted towards her?"

But how will the Westerners be taught that the Orthodox Church is the One and True Church when they see her consorting with the false "churches" as an equal among equals? Will they not think, therefore, that Orthodoxy is also like the others — relative and partial? Or is it reasonable for one to hope that those councils of fanatic biretta-wearers and befrocked pastors will ever be able to recognize the truth? They are only flattering the Orthodox in order to draw them over to their side. If they had a genuine nostalgia to know Orthodoxy, they would have no need for councils and conferences. They would have gone to drink from her sources, from her Fathers and Saints.

No! the best way to convince others of the truth is to believe in it yourself. Do not discuss it, only confess it. The councils and

non-Orthodox) are prayed for by the priest in the secret prayers after the Epiclesis. The whole petition therefore prays "For the good estate of the holy (local Orthodox) churches of God and for the union of all the faithful (through the Eucharist in Christ), let us pray to the Lord." Fr. Michael Gelsinger has rightly translated the phrase from Greek to read "all the faithful." (Editors' note)

conferences debate the truth. But this is a betrayal, because in such instances it is not a matter of dialogue with and admonition to heretics, but of discussion with "churches." Christ does not ask for debaters, but for confessors. The truth which He taught us is not the kind that is debatable. In the various ecumenical conferences the discussion takes the form of commerce, where an exchange of compromises takes place in matters of faith in order to arrive at a final agreement. Under such conditions even the mere attendance of an Orthodox at an ecumenical conference is a betrayal of Christ. It is the betrayal of Christ to unbelievers for thirty pieces of silver, because by attending, the Orthodox admits his Faith to be debatable, and permits the notion that he too will make compromises if he is given a satisfactory exchange.

If, instead of this, all those who speak of union today would confess Orthodoxy as the only and absolute truth and refuse every official and unofficial ecclesiastical contact with heretics, without fearing to name them as such, then their voice would be heard much farther; and more important, it would be respected and would provoke thought. Whereas now their voice is a voice of compromises, a voice which does not move anyone, a voice which, deep down, no one respects.

The Fathers did not enter into discussions with heretics. They confessed the truth and refuted their claims without courteousness and compliments. They never arrived at mutual understandings with heretical "churches." Their dialogue was always public and had a view to the salvation and edification of souls. The Orthodox Church did not converse with "churches" of the heretics. It was not a discussion of the Church with churches, but a dialogue between the Church and souls who had lost their way. The Church does not discuss, for she does not seek. She simply gives — because she has everything.

IV. SALVATION FROM THE WORLD

But why are our Christians so easily moved by sermons about the union of the churches? And instead of being filled with zeal for the transmission of the truth to this world which lacks it so much, they suck on the caramel of peace, weighing to see which are more, the things which separate or those which unite Christians. It is because they themselves lack knowledge of the truth. Most of them being members of social-Christian organizations and brotherhoods, were catechized from their earliest years in an ethico-philosophical system with a Christian veneer which led them to believe that the purpose of Christianity is to achieve the peaceful coexistence of men in the spirit of love. Eternity and the vision of God are things very distant for these Christians, and often of no interest. Most of them, being extroverts, are men of action who came to Christianity to find an organized and directed *modus vivendi,* a way of living as good and honorable citizens upon this earth. For such people, God is the Great Servant of their personal interests, and eternal life is a good but, fortunately, distant hope of restoration.

In Christians such as these, the sermons about union take root very easily. How good it would be, really, if the circle of our own honest and virtuous people were to be extended on a world-wide scale. We could have transactions without fear of perhaps being fooled; we could have good and peaceful relations without ever being in danger of persecution or of having to struggle. As for the truth, "What is truth?" We all believe in Christ, that is sufficient. Besides, the world today faces difficult times. Christians must be united quickly to face communism, for example. They ask, "Who will guide and who will save this contemporary world? Only a single, united Christian Church," they reply.

But Christ did not become man in order to save this world which abides in wickedness. Rather, He came to save His own from the world, to pull them away from the ranks of the evil one, to unite them to Himself and to deify them by grace, and with them to save the entire groaning creation. The world is walking the way of death. It is following the ruler of this world, the enemy of God. "I do not pray for the world, but for those whom Thou hast given Me" (John 9:17).

But such people take the part of the world and sacrifice the jewels of the Christian faith and life for that diabolical party which will never be saved. It is not Christ Who asks for the so-called union of the churches, but the world. Christ does not ask for the union of falsehood with truth, but it is the world that seeks to adulterate the truth, to make it relative and partial. This is why, when a discussion arises about the union of the churches, one sees that it is supported enthusiastically by people who were never previously interested in matters of religion. Union is the best way of neutralizing Christianity that the devil's party has discovered. It is the beginning of the dissolution of Christianity and its submission to the whims of politics; it is the conversion of Christianity into a servant of the interests of the world.

With union, Christianity may acquire greater world power, but it will lose all its spiritual strength, exactly what troubles the world. Has it not already happened to the Roman Catholic "Church"? The Papists' thirst for world power has made them descend to the well-worn path of political machinations, from which they have emerged as tools of the great political trends.

All those who speak of union have not understood why Christ came into the world. They think that He came to preach an artificial ethical message like their own, that He came to teach us how to live upon this earth as good citizens. They say over and over again that people must follow the law of Christ in order that the Kingdom of God might finally come upon the earth. Some speak of a "Christian Greece," others, of "Christian democracies," others of "Christian kingdoms," and none of them realize how much their expectations resemble the expectations of the Jews who wanted the Messiah to be an earthly king.

They do not want Christ as He is; they do not want the Christ Who refused to submit to the devil's temptations in the desert. They want a Christ Who will submit to them. They want a Christ Who desires the kingdoms of the earth, a Christ Who will turn the stones into bread so that men may be satiated, a Christ who will overwhelm the world with miracles that inspire awe and constrain men to submit.

In other words, these people do not wait for Christ, but for the Antichrist. Until the Second Coming, Christ will remain humble and hidden, far from earthly powers and earthly comforts, without forcing anyone to follow Him, and only asking of those who would come near Him to resemble Him in humility and obscurity, and to expect nothing earthly.

The "Christians" who speak of a "nation of God," "Christian

Greece," "world Christianity," and "union of the churches" do not want that kind of Christ. Like the Grand Inquisitor of Dostoyevsky, they are ready to cast Christ into the fire because He upsets their plans which they have been persistently cultivating for years. "You came and taught us a Christianity which is inhuman and hard," says the Inquisitor to Christ, "and we've labored for so many centuries now to make it a human religion. And now that we've succeeded, you've come to spoil our efforts of so many centuries? But you won't accomplish it. Tomorrow I shall order them to burn you as a heretic."

Yes, people want a Christ Who will talk about this life and not the other, a Christ Who will offer the pleasures of this life and not of the next. They do not want wealth that cannot be weighed and touched, but wealth that is tangible here and now. They do not want Him as ruler of the future age, but of the present one.

This is why they do not care what will become of the truth when the wavering and so-called Christian churches unite after a thousand and one compromises. This is why they are not interested in what will become of the life in Christ after the invasion of the clean land of Orthodoxy by so many religious barbarians and spiritual nitwits. The truth does not interest them; Christ does not interest them, nor the life in the Spirit and grace. They are interested only in the earthly power that unity gives and world rule under a single world-view.

These people want to be called Christians without really being Christians. Most of them believe that they are true Christians, because they do not know what Christianity is and confuse it with philosophical theories and "world theories," to use a favorite term of theirs. In actuality, they are followers of the Antichrist like the Jews of Christ's times, like the Jews of every age.

The Jews awaited the Messiah for centuries, and when He came they did not accept Him; instead, they hung Him on the Cross. And why? Because Christ was not what they were waiting for. And that is why they were not able to recognize the Messiah in His person. They were waiting for an earthly king, a world conqueror. They awaited someone who would subject all the races of the world at the feet of the nation of Israel, who would force the Roman rulers of the world to bow and worship him, who would give power and glory to his followers.

When they saw Him poor and humble, meek and full of peace, one Who offered no earthly goods but spoke of heavenly things, and not only that, but even asked them to deny the earthly and tangible so that liberated they could reach the heavenly and intangible, they realized that He was not for them. He was not the Messiah they awaited, but exactly the opposite. He Who refused to turn the stones into bread for all to be filled, Who refused to overwhelm the mobs with His power and did not agree to subjugate the kingdoms of the earth, was not the appropriate leader for them. That is why they crucified Him and began awaiting another. And they still await him. And along with the Jews are millions of people awaiting the Messiah of the Jews, and most of them are called Christians. And they have no idea that they await the same Messiah as the Jews.

V. THE ANTICHRIST

The tragedy is that the Messiah whom the Jews await will come. It was said by the mouth of Christ and by the mouth of the Apostles; it is written in the books of the New Testament. The Messiah of the Jews shall come. He will give the bread which Christ refused to give, and along with that, all the material things which He refused to give. He will overwhelm them with signs and wonders which people unto the ends of the earth will fear and be amazed at, and they will come grovelling to fall at his feet. He will unite all the nations and races and kingdoms of the world into one state. He will fill the hearts of the Scribes of the law and the Pharisees with joy —the hearts of every race of "Jews." Yes, the Messiah of the Jews shall come. He will be what Christ is not, and he will not be what Christ is. He will be the Antichrist.

"Children, it is the last hours, and as ye have heard that the Antichrist cometh . . ." (I John 2:18).

"Now we beseech you, brethren, by the coming of our Lord Jesus Christ and by our gathering together unto Him, that ye be not shaken in mind or be troubled, neither by spirit, nor by word, nor by letter as from us, as that the day of Christ is at hand. Let no man deceive you by any means, for that day shall not come except there come a falling away first, and that man of sin be revealed, the son of perdition, who opposeth and exalteth himself above all that is called God or that is worshipped; so that he as God sitteth in the temple of God, showing himself that he is God. Remember ye not, that when I was yet with you, I told you these things? And now ye know what withholdeth that he might be revealed in his time. For the mystery of iniquity already doth work, only until he who withholdeth be taken out of the way. And then shall the wicked one be revealed, whom the Lord shall consume by the breath of His mouth and by the brightness of His coming shall destroy him, him whose coming is according to the working of Satan with all power and signs and false wonders and with every deception of unrighteousness in them that perish, because they received not the love of the truth that they might be saved. And for this cause God shall send them a working of delusion that they should believe a lie, that they all might be judged who believed not the truth but had pleasure in unrighteousness" (II Thess. 2:1-12).

The Antichrist will not appear in history with a fearful and shocking manner by which all would recognize him, nor will he have an ugly appearance, nor yet will he do immoral works. He will come in such a way that very few will realize who he is. He will come after a long preparation of centuries which started in the first days of the Church and which continues with increasing progress in our days. Humanity will see in his person its greatest benefactor.

So many centuries of apostasy have cultivated humanity and have prepared it to accept him. Humanity awaits him as its ideal leader. All the developments of history lead to the Antichrist.

VI. THE MYSTERY OF INIQUITY

Catholicism permitted the worldly spirit to nourish the Christianity of the West. It steeped Christian thought in the rationalism and the pagan disposition of the ancient Greeks. Finally, with the Infallibility of the Pope, Catholicism brought a mechanical element into the relation between God and man, teaching that God promised to speak through the mouth of sinful and haughty men, as many of the Popes have been. The Renaissance and humanism were the completion of the Western Christian world's turn toward idolatry. In reality these were manifestations of men's disillusionment with an adulterated Christianity. Today humanism has become the religion of the age, unfortunately preached even by so-called Christains as "Hellenic-Christian" civilization.

Protestantism drew Papist rationalism to its extreme conclusions. Protestantism rejected the holiness of the Church and her guidance by the Holy Spirit because it saw neither holiness nor truth in the "church" of the West. Thus it abolished Tradition and left its believers with no criterion of truth or falsehood, estranging the grace of God from its realm forever.

From Protestantism to atheism and materialism, there was no longer a great distance. Many kinds of philosophies began to lay claim to the position of Christian faith in the minds of men, and in the end scientism conquered the world. It had a special power of winning over the masses because its achievements in the field of technology evoked the wonder and rapture of the masses, which, lacking spiritual criteria, fell an easy prey to materialism. Science further gave humanity the false sense of knowledge. It may have changed its views and theories at every moment, but each time these views and theories had the sanctity of proven knowledge; and that influences peoples' minds in a magic way.

Finally, when humanity, having descended by such steps, became enslaved to the passion of materialism, communism sprang forth. When people even came to believe that the only real good is money, it was natural to demand its equitable distribution from governments which were apathetic towards the pain of the impoverished people. This demand filled souls with hate and malice and made them even more unhappy, opening unbridgeable chasms between people and leading many to the hate of Cain. (Whatever we write here does not mean that the fair distribution of money is not an obligation, and a rather fundamental one, of government.) That is how the war started between capitalism and communism, which are actually two sister systems identically materialistic and money-worshipping, and divided only by their own interests and the battle over the distribution. The program of both is to turn stones into bread, to unite the world under their influence, and to astonish the world with accomplishments that man could not even imagine. Thus humanity has gradually reached the outer gates of the Antichrist's kingdom. It has arrived at the point where it has not only the will, but also the ability to respond positively to the three temptations of Lucifer. In a little while, all that will remain will be for the Antichrist himself to take over the general leadership of the universal state, to do away with hunger and poverty forever, and to provide men abundantly with material goods so that in their hearts, filled with pleasure and comfort, there will no longer be a place for God.

VII. UNION OF RELIGIONS

When one considers all this, he realizes that in a humanity concerned with nothing else but its own tranquility, which holds nothing sacred and holy but its own materialistic interests, that in a world of pragmatic men who regard any discussion concerning truth as useless babbling, not only is the union of the churches not difficult, but on the contrary, it is inevitable. Moreover, I dare say that not only is the union of the so–called Christian churches inevitable, but the union of all religions generally.

In his kingdom the Antichrist will not tolerate discord; he will not tolerate religions or quarrels over religious questions. He will sit in the temple of God as God, and all the people of the earth will worship him, because "power was given him over every race and people and tongue and nation. And all that dwell upon the earth shall worship him, whose names are not written in the book of life" (Rev. 12:7-8). For those people, then, "whose names are not written in the book of life," only one religion will exist, the religion of the Antichrist.

Already, right now there are specimens of religions such as can comprehend all religions — forerunners of the religion of the Antichrist. One such religion is Freemasonry. It has already been embraced by the more progressive of the world's leaders. With its syncretism it can reconcile in the minds of fools all the religious antitheses of humanity and overcome all the obstacles and difficulties to union which the various churches will meet. What reason is there, indeed, for exerting so much effort to find acceptable solutions for dogmatic and other differences between the various denominations, and afterwards for the differences between religions, and not for advancing directly to the union of all religions? To a kind of Freemasonry?

And having realized this, most of today's religious leaders, at least the "greatest" and most "important," have hot-footed it (progressive as they are) to become Masons, without its preventing them from wearing their cassocks or vestments, or from celebrating their Liturgies. But because the laity are not quite ready yet, it is necessary that the former keep up appearances and proceed first to union of the churches, and then to union of the religions.

VIII. A GLANCE INTO THE PAST

These, then, will be the developments in the not-so-distant future. That is why the Lord asks whether He will find any faithful when He comes to the earth again. "When the Son of man cometh, shall He find faith on the earth?" (Luke 18:8).

A glance into the past will teach us much about the course ecclesiastical matters have taken and will take.

The Byzantine emperors' first tendencies to unify with Papal error fortunately were cut off by the attitude of the people and the subjugation of Byzantium to the Turks. But as soon as the Greek nation found its liberty, the old temptation knocked at its door again. In the beginning, the true Greeks, men of the people and of the traditions, resisted the current of Europeanization. But they were unlettered, and even though they had shed their blood for the freedom of their land, they were quickly pushed aside by the newly arrived men of letters who, along with the self-conceit which half-learning creates, had the power of King Otto's court. "These degraded the fatherland and the religion which is now shaken by the irreligious. In the time of Turkish occupation, not one stone from the old churches was disturbed. But these deceivers joined their interests with the contaminated Phanariotes and the like who were contaminated in Europe, and they spoiled our monasteries and churches, befouling some and turning others into stables. We suffered these things from many such priests, and from laymen, military men, and politicians. Even though we shed our blood, we are in danger of losing our fatherland and our religion" (Macriyiannis, *Memoirs,* p. 398).

These half-educated intellectuals scorned the Greek people with the passion of fifth columnists. They disdained their language, their customs and manners, and their mentality. They used all possible means at their disposal to adulterate the truth of their Faith and to graft secularism and rationalism onto the holy tree of Orthodoxy, which for so many centuries remained undefiled under the barbarian conqueror. To strike the Church at her heart, they struck at her monasteries. They closed some, confiscated the property of others, and to others they sent "progressive" abbots who dissolved them more easily than any double-edged sword of state.

Without her monasteries, and with her bishops enslaved to the state, the Church became an unfenced vineyard. The education of the nation left the Church's hands and fell into the hands of a humanistic state which, with all its hypocrisies about a Hellenic-Christian civilization, was and remains completely pagan. Everything began to be adapted to the taste of the *nouveau riche* and provincial Athenian society.

The worship of the Church began to deteriorate to something more worldly. Byzantine music began to be Europeanized and degenerated into theatrical four-part harmony. The icons began to look too austere and ugly to the eyes of the women of the "upper" classes, who wanted "sweet Jesuses" full of indulgence for their iniquities, incapable of evoking awe and reverence. The beards and long hair of the clergy began to bother them, and the clergy, responsive to the demands of the contemporary public, began to groom themselves. The lowly and sanctified little candle with its contrite atmosphere was replaced by Edison's lights, making the church resemble an imperial hall appropriate for the weddings and official appearances of the ruling class.

But that was not all. Not only primary and secondary but also higher education left the hands of the Church. Thus the theologians, future priests, and hierarchs were not born in the bosom of the Church, their natural mother, but in the bosom of a state university full of the stench of rationalism and spiritual shallowness, without any possibility of tasting of the mystical life of holiness in Christ, which alone makes true theologians. And so there sprouted up, like tares in the Church, theologians who had their minds filled with many philosophical theories of Protestant or Roman origin, but their hearts empty of the life of Orthodoxy.

These people were incapable of seeing the chasm that divides the Eastern Church from the Western "churches." They considered it only a question of dogmatic formulas, not a matter of life and essence. For them life in Christ was a series of emotional states and ethical acts, just as it is for Westerners. The revelation (the inner vision) of God, the living experience of the presence of Christ, and the indwelling of the Holy Spirit, that is, the abiding of truth in a man's heart, were unknown to them. When they speak of truth, they mean a cut-and-dried dogma. Dogma, however, for them as for the Westerners, was a separate world of intellectual formulas, burdensome enough, and whose value, after this split between life and faith, they were incapable of appreciating.

The foundations, then, upon which even our most well-intentioned theologians were going to build in order to defend their Orthodoxy, were rotten to the core. It is frightening when one considers that the whole of contemporary Greek religious life is built upon these rotten foundations. At one time the piety of the people sprang from the monasteries, which were its spiritual bulwark and guide; in the Greek Kingdom piety came to be founded on the theologian, lay or clerical, whom we have described. This theologian, imitating Western examples, organized brotherhoods and Christian unions and took preaching and catechism into his own hands. And whereas before, the piety of a place had as its center the local monastery and the priests of the Church, and the Christian of Area A did not differ in any way from the Christian of Area B because all were children of the same Orthodox Church, now the theologian organized factions; and now in one and the same place there are Christians of Faction A and Christians of Faction B, always rivals and distrusting, divided — without either side understanding what their differences are. But in spite of all the hate and schisms between them, the factions agree that as far as the Westerners are concerned, "there are more things uniting us than there are separating us," and "we must look to the things which unite us and overlook those which separate us." In other words, they regard union and love with their Western "brothers" (whom they have never seen or known) easier than with their Orthodox compatriots and neighbors, whom they see daily and know. As we have said, today people labor for the love of man, for the abstract love of humanity, at the same moment that they are incapable of loving their neighbor.

IX. THE OLD CALENDAR QUESTION

In this atmosphere of deterioration, there suddenly came, after pressure from the state, the first official step of the Greek Church towards the Pope: the adoption of the Papal calendar.

Unfortunately, few have understood the significance of the "old calendar" issue, as the matter is called. Most attribute the resistance of the Old Calendarists to the narrow-mindedness of the uneducated, this being another indication of the deep contempt nurtured by the conceited educated towards the unlearned. But in order for these uneducated people to resist the way they did, they must have had, if nothing else, a religious zeal and spiritual concern lacking in the masses of the indifferent who, not knowing the true nature of the problem, followed the majority of the hierarchy. None of the enlightened theologians and their followers even showed any indication of pain over the division of the Greek Church, nor did any of them seek to answer the painful cries of so many thousands of faithful. The majority were on their side; their numbers always gave them a sense of security. In actuality, though, they did not even have the numbers on their side. For although there were only a few thousand Old Calendarists and millions of followers of the new calendar, those few thousands were thousands of faithful suffering for the Church. Whereas among the millions of the indifferent, the materialists and atheists, followers of the new calendar, it is doubtful that one could find a few thousand really faithful people. They only sneered at those simple new confessors of Orthodoxy, saying that they refused out of superstition to correct their calendar which is not accurate.

But the problem did not lie there. They were unjustified in accusing the Old Calendarists of fighting over a calendar. The issue was not over which of the two calendars is correct. It is a known fact that both calendars are inaccurate. Neither had the Old Calendarists insisted on the old calendar, nor had the New Calendarists brought forth the new calendar, for reasons of astronomical accuracy. The reason that prompted the decision for the introduction of the new calendar into Greece was neither astronomical nor theological. It simply involved one of the many capitulations of the state-enslaved hierarchy to its lord, which asked it of them in order to facilitate its business transactions.

The reason for the Old Calendarist refusal to comply was very theological and sprang from a deep ecclesiastical consciousness. Actually, the liturgical unity of the Church was risked in favor of political interests. With the change of the calendar there followed a severance of the liturgical accord between the Greek Church and the other Orthodox Churches, which preserve the old calendar to this day. And it was not only a matter of discord in the liturgical life of the militant Church — the continuity of the liturgical life of the militant Church with the triumphant also was broken.

In Greece when the church bells call the faithful to celebrate Christmas and the chanters chant joyfully the "Christ is born, glorify ye," millions of our Orthodox brothers throughout the rest of the world and on the Holy Mountain are still in the fast of Advent; and they do not hear the bells, nor chant with us the joyful hymns of Christmas.

Can one imagine anything worse for the Church than this break in liturgical concord which estranges us spiritually not only from other Orthodox but from all the Orthodox who preceded us, from the triumphant Church of those who have fallen asleep in Christ, and from the Saints who celebrated and performed the Liturgy according to the old calendar which we rejected?

So many efforts of our Fathers, so many synods were needed to enact that festal calendar — and all this so that there would be liturgical harmony between the Christian churches, because this harmony and accord expresses the internal liturgical unity of the Church. This is what makes the Church visibly one, despite the multiplicity of local churches. The Church is not made one the way the Pope thinks, by hard discipline and obedience to a prescribed hierarchy which has as its head a single individual who claims to replace Christ on earth, but the Church is made one by the mystical communion in the Body and Blood of Christ. Every church where the Holy Eucharist is performed and where the faithful are gathered "in the same place" comprises the whole image of the One, Holy, Catholic, and Apostolic Church. What makes one parish comprise one body with all other parishes, and one diocese comprise one body with all other dioceses, is the mystical communion of all in the Body and Blood of Christ in the Holy Spirit and truth.

The unity of the Church, therefore, is a mystical bond which is forged during the Holy Eucharist when the faithful partake of the Body and Blood of Christ. Christians are one body, those who live upon the earth today and those who have lived before us in past centuries, and also those who will live in the years to come; and this is because we have a common root, the Body of Christ. "We many are one bread, one body, for we all partake of the one Bread."

The unity of the Church, therefore, is not administrative, is not disciplinary or organizational, but liturgical. That is why the festal calendar is so important. The unity which springs from the Holy Eucharist, the one Faith, and the one Baptism ceases to be manifested externally when there is liturgical anarchy. The form and the words of the Liturgy have been prescribed so that all the churches can worship God in the same way. And the service book for each month *(Menaion)* contains the daily hymns commemorating the Saints of the day and the chants for every holy day. In this way no discord can disrupt the liturgical harmony. Even the music and the iconography, which are called liturgical arts, have similarly been prescribed so that no icon painter or chanter can paint an icon or chant according to his own imagination, but is compelled to adapt his personal skill and ability to prototypes of the most austere spiritual realism. And similarly, the calendar of festivals has been prescribed in order that no priest can celebrate the holy days whenever he wishes, but that there be complete communion of prayer among all the faithful upon the earth.

Therefore, what the artist does who paints the icons of the Church according to his own tastes, disdaining the Tradition, and what the chanter does who destroys the liturgical harmony by singing theatrically in church instead of chanting, the Greek hierarchs have likewise done, spoiling the liturgical harmony of the Orthodox Church by deciding to follow a different calendar of festivals in Greece than that which the other Orthodox churches and the Holy Mountain of Athos follow. Thus on the Holy Mountain they celebrate a different Saint and chant different hymns than they do in Thessalonika; the Transfiguration of the Lord is celebrated on one day in Athens and on another in Jerusalem, Sinai, and Moscow.

The tragedy of this discord is difficult to conceive of in this country [i.e., Greece] because of the distances. But it becomes painfully perceptible to one who travels to Europe and sees in the neighborhoods of the same city the Russians celebrating one holiday and the Greeks another, or one hears the bells of the Greek church calling the faithful while the bells of the Russian church remain silent. And then one asks himself if both churches are Orthodox.

It has not been realized in Greece how serious a compromise with the elements of the world and how serious a blow against the Church was the abolition of the old calendar in favor of the new. And if a few did understand, they did not have the strength to raise their stature and proclaim the truth. No one of worldly wisdom and strength found the words to protest. Thus it was proved once again that "God has chosen the weak of the world to shame the strong," and that "God hath made foolish the wisdom of the wise," because whereas the wise were silent and accepted it, the uneducated faithful were aroused. And they "spake not foolishness as did the foolish wise of the world." They did not resort to astronomical theories and mathematical calculations, but they spoke in the name of Tradition, which they felt was something holy which no one can trample upon in favor of science which continually rejects its own theories, or in favor of the political and economic interests of a country.

But "the disciples of the wise men of this world consider those taught by God fools." Thus from the beginning until today, they consider the Old Calendarists fools, religious fanatics, superstitious, etc., and they rejoice at their own knowledge which places them above such "trifles" so that they do not make issues out of "nothing."

X. THE UNRAVELING

But when you reckon one element of Tradition as trivial, then at the first opportunity you will consider trivial whatever other things you do not like in the Tradition. That is what happened with the iconography; that is what happened with the psalmody; that is what happened with the appearance of the priests. Now the robes seem too black for them; later the beards and the hair will seem too long. They want to put musical instruments in the church. They do away with the stalls on the sides of the church and replace them with comfortable pews. They revile monasticism, slander the monks, confiscate the properties of the monasteries, carry on systematic propaganda against monasticism. They overlook the canons which forbid joint prayer with heretics; they attend their conferences and pray together with them. They are indifferent to the opinion of the people in the election of bishops and priests. They shorten the Liturgy and cut out sections from the services "so that people won't get tired." In other words, they change the Orthodox customs according to the tastes of a decadent society full of the worship of the flesh and materialism.

In this way the fabric of the Tradition begins to unravel, and no one knows where it will stop or if it will stop. And besides, this unraveling is so easy today because it has the approval of the world, of the influential, and of the educated. The educated especially consider it their honor not to agree with the Fathers of the Church, but to agree with a certain great, scholarly professor of Protestant theology or with a certain Jesuit professor who is famous in Europe, and so on.

How then shall the Orthodox Tradition and Faith not be adulterated? And how, under such conditions, shall we not discuss the union of the churches and not consider it something which can easily be accomplished? Is it then difficult for an "Orthodox" church which has acquired the same mentality and the same dispositions as the Western "churches" to be united with them? Is the day far off when we shall go to church on Sunday and hear the priest praying: "and for our Father the Pope of Rome"? Will anyone react if such a thing happens? Or will it seem natural to all that we have finally jumped over the differences which separate East and West?

XI. GOD IS NOT MOCKED

But let all who speak so lightly about the union of the churches understand that the unity of the Church is a mystical gift of the divine presence. It is not something which is decided upon at conferences, but something which either exists or does not exist. No decision of men can constrain God.

Of course, externally union can come about, and all can declare — Protestants, Catholics, and Orthodox — that now we are at last one church, and we can commemorate the Pope of Rome, and the Pope of Rome can commemorate the Patriarch of Constantinople. If we all agree upon one "minimum of truth," upon one simplified creed, and if a few other issues are settled there can be union. It will be a legally and externally valid system, but it will be a system that has no relation with the Church of Christ, even if all the external appearances make it resemble the Church. "God is not mocked." When the conditions of His presence do not exist in men, God does not come to men.

The Church of Christ was never a human system. The Church was born, it was not made. The discussions of men can make something to which they can give the name "Church." But this fabrication will be something with no life. The living Church will have no relation to it. She will exist somewhere far from all these fabrications, unaltered, full of truth and light, pure of every falsehood of compromises, with the Holy Spirit lighting her steps and enveloping her like the light of the sun, guiding her "to the fulness of truth."

As for how many true Christians there will be, it does not matter, even if they can be counted on one hand. They will be the bearers of the Tradition, which they will not simply have learned, but have lived, having had its living experience. Christians live in the Tradition as in an element, as fish live in water.

Let all who truly seek God stop talking about the union of the "churches." The Church does not admit of union because she was never broken. Men leave her, even if they retain many of her external marks. Let all who love God return to the Church and humble themselves that they may enter, because her gate is narrow and one must bend very low in order to pass through.

XII. THE INFALLIBLE CRITERION

But in the chaos and hypocrisy of the contemporary world, it is not easy to discern the Church of Christ and to draw near her, because it is not sufficient for a church to be named Orthodox in order to be such literally. Unfortunately, apostasy exists even under the externally Orthodox cassock, and under Orthodox domes, and among the practicing Orthodox people. But this is nothing new; the

Church knew it from her first steps, but now it has reached unusual dimensions.

We must learn to discern the Church behind appearances. As far as appearances are concerned, in the Orthodox Church today confusion and chaos prevail externally. Everyone — educated or uneducated, believer or unbeliever — has his own view of what Christianity or Orthodoxy is and supports his view fanatically. And in this storm it is impossible to find your course without a compass. There is one infallible criterion: the continuation of Tradition. Wherever the Tradition is preserved living and pure without disruption or change from the times of the Apostles, as many faithful — bishops, priests, or laymen — live and transmit this Tradition, there is the Orthodox Church, and they constitute the Body of Christ. All others, priests or laymen, who wish to be called Orthodox without following the living Tradition of the centuries are intruders; they are tares in Christ's field.

Today the tares are very many and the ears of wheat very few, but the field is God's field, and in spite of the variety of tares, the wheat remains the same from generation to generation, from seed to seed, the same as that first wheat which the Holy Spirit planted in that same divine field on the day of Pentecost.

That living Tradition has never been disrupted, because the very mouth of Christ promised the Church that "the gates of Hades shall not prevail against her," and the mouth of God does not lie. Those who search to find the Tradition of the Christian Church of the first centuries or of the centuries before the schism in order to follow it confess that they have lost the continuity of Tradition. But they are never going to find it no matter how much they push forward their researches, because the Tradition is something living and transmitted as life from the living to the living. It is not something which is discovered through scholarly studies, nor is it something which is learned intellectually.

XIII. HIDDEN BUT LIVING

Those millions of tares which have sprung up in the bosom of the Orthodox Church in recent times have brought a secular spirit with them, so that no Orthodox Church has been able to keep her outward marks unchanged. Even the Old Calendarists, who have kept such a good line in the calendar issue, in the case of iconography clearly bear stigmas of betrayal of the Tradition. This fact is a common sin of all the Orthodox churches of late.

Fortunately up to now, all the deviations from the Tradition which we have described have not cut off the Orthodox churches from their root. The tree remains alive and thriving in spite of all the garnishes which they have added to it. The Orthodox churches have not withered as has happened to the "churches" of the West. If you just shake off the dust which the secular spirit has scattered upon them, you will find the fresh leaves of the authentic Tradition. Tradition has never ceased to live and to be in force in the sphere of Orthodoxy. There are still monks who live Orthodox monasticism. There are still genuine theologians who have not defiled the truth, but keep it shining and pure, far from every alien mingling. There are still Byzantine chanters and true bearers of the Orthodox iconographic tradition. There are still priests like the old ones dedicated to their sacred function, whose constant contact with God does not permit them to be distressed over their long beards and black robes, but rather makes these things radiate holiness. There are still simple people who are worthy of seeing great miracles.*

The true Tradition, then — the life, the spiritual experience, and the teaching of the Apostles and the Holy Fathers of all ages, these imprints of the walking of the Holy Spirit in the hearts of Christians — exists and continues alive among the living without any break from the Apostolic times. There is a constant harmony in all the actions of Orthodox of all ages up to the present day, written and unwritten; and this is the golden rule upon which everyone must measure his thoughts and actions in order to see if he is within or out of the scope of Orthodoxy. The outward signs might give the impression that the continuity has been corrupted or broken, but if one looks a little further he will see that it still blossoms and refreshes those who seek it.

The Tradition exists and will continue to exist until the end of

* See *A Great Sign* by Photios Kontoglou, published in Greek by "Astir," which describes the amazing events in Mytilene, when in these last days the Saints Raphael, Nicholas, and many others have revealed their lives and relics five hundred years after their martyrdoms.

the world. But every passing day makes its discovery more difficult. Every passing day adds more garnish upon the tree of Orthodoxy, and that is how people become confused and do not know where the truth lies.

XIV. THE ARK

Someday sooner or later, no one knows exactly when, the "churches" and the religions will be united. In that chaos of falsehood even the chosen will be in danger of losing their way. It will be the age of the Antichrist.

How and when the Antichrist will come, no one can say. And it is unknown how many shall be able to recognize him when he comes, because he will come as a benefactor of humanity. For the present, one thing can be said with certainty: all these movements towards union among nations and churches, all these compromises, all this uniformity of humanity gradually produced under the steamroller of technological culture are paving the way for the coming of the Antichrist.

This development of humanity, according to the criteria of the world, is wonderful. But according to Christian criteria, it is a development towards destruction.

This does not surprise or frighten the Christian. He knows that the world has condemned itself. And that is why Christ refused to pray for the world. "I do not ask for the world." The ruler of this world is the devil, and the devil "from the beginning was a murderer."

Death will find the world at the height of its glory, at the height of self-conceit, at the summit of the tower of Babel, when man will be at the zenith of his very old attempt to become god by his own powers, apart from God. When the Son of man comes, he shall find man in the full glory of his satanic mania.

God does not ask the Christian to save the world. Any attempt on the part of Christians to change the course the world has taken would be futile and ridiculous. The world is a sinking ship, and it is sinking because its very structure is rotten. God does not ask the Christian to save the ship, but to save as many of the shipwrecked as he can.

The new Ark of Noe, the Church of Christ, sails near the site of the shipwreck. Any who wish to be saved from the waters must seek refuge in her. But in order to find refuge they must forsake the world, not so much geographically as essentially. "Wherefore come out from among them and be ye separate, saith the Lord, and touch not any unclean thing, and I will receive you" (II Cor. 6:17).

But here is where the difficulties begin. How can you forsake the world when your whole life is bound up in it? But to answer this question is not the purpose of the present book. One finds it in the Holy Scriptures and the Fathers. Besides, the whole life in Christ is a struggle for freedom from the world, from the "Egypt" of the passions, and for refuge in the Ark of the Church.

But when the age of the Antichrist approaches, even the Ark of the Church shall be difficult to discern. Many will say, "Behold, here is Christ," and "There is Christ," but they will be false prophets. Whatever will be accepted officially as the Church, having little by little already betrayed the treasures of the Faith, will have been assimilated by the indescribable, unifying marmelade which will retain most of the outward signs of the Church with satanic cleverness. Here and there small groups of faithful with some priest will still preserve the true Tradition alive.

But who will be able to recognize the Church of Christ in those small, scorned groups of faithful that lack all worldly splendor? Yet at the end of time the One, Holy, Catholic, and Apostolic Church will be just those forgotten and outwardly disunited little parishes which may even be ignorant of the others' existence, but will be united among themselves by the mystical bonds of the Body and Blood of the Lord, in the Holy Spirit, with the common Faith and Tradition which they will preserve undefiled.

In those days even the chosen will be in danger of being led astray. Much courage is needed for one to side with the few and to go against the currents of the world, with the danger of being ridiculed by the "smart" and abused by the strong. Much wisdom is needed in order for one to discern the truth there exactly where the whole world sees nonsense and stupidity. Besides, the followers of falsehood will have the miracle on their side, the miracle which the devil asked of Christ in the desert, the signs and wonders of the false prophets and the false Christs. "For there shall arise false

Christs and false prophets, and they shall show great signs and wonders; insomuch that if it were possible, they shall deceive the very elect" (Mat. 24:24). How many shall be able to find their way when all the beacons will be misguiding? Then, "he who persists to the end shall be saved."

XV. THE MASKS

For the present, let all who wish to live near Christ hasten to acquire discretion in order to recognize beforehand the false prophets and false Christs, and let them wear the armor of the Faith so that they will be able to strike them and their followers invincibly.

For our age is a cunning age, where falsehood is disguised and poison is offered sugar-coated, where the roads are full of snares and well-camouflaged pits. Whoever is misled by appearances is lost.

We must learn to distinguish the Church from the world, for the destiny of the Church is one thing and that of the world another. We must have as much distrust of the world as we have faith in the Church, as much hate towards the world (not towards men, but the world) as we have love for the Church, as much pessimism for the world as we have optimism for the Church.

The world is the camp, the mentality, and the intentions of those who have rejected the offering of God, who have turned their backs when He wanted to speak to them, who have separated themselves from Him forever. These people have given preference to death over life. They are not punished, just as the demons are not punished, for no one wishes them any harm. Of their own accord they chose death, of their own accord they chose to be enemies of God and to stand far away from Him.

This choice is made in life, independent of moments and time, in the depths of our heart, and it is irrevocable. Freedom separates the spiritual beings into two camps. There are two types of people, as there are two types of angels: the friends of God and the enemies of God.

Freedom does not lie in individual actions, but in the whole inclination and disposition of man, in the final positive or negative response to God's call. Freedom lies in the general direction of man's life, and not in the details of that life.

The details are deceiving; they make the Pharisees and Scribes appear to be friends of God, and the thief, the harlot, the publican, and Saul [Paul] appear to be His enemies.

We must be able to recognize the true enemies and the true friends of God under the masks of hypocrisy or weakness.

We are in an age where the masks of hypocrisy have multiplied and reached an astonishing degree of perfection. From one moment to the next we are in danger of being deceived by men who, while wearing the mask of the friends of God, are actually His enemies.

Such are those who speak of the union of the churches. They are the Church's most dangerous enemies, the false prophets of the Gospel.

The enemies who appear without any mask — the atheists, the materialists, the communists — cannot fool anyone. They are the ones who can kill the body but cannot kill the soul. But the others —"Orthodox" patriarchs, bishops and archbishops, leaders of Christian organizations, theologians and professors of theology — all who speak with hypocritical Christian love for our "brothers" the heretics and spread the message of union, all of these mask-wearers may not be killing the body, but they are surely killing the soul. This is why the battle against them must be relentless.

CHAPTER TWO

XVI. CONTEMPORARY IDOLATRY

And now let us see who are those Europeans with whom they want us to be united as a state and as a Church?

A frightening antinomy characterizes the Europeans: it is the antithesis between the inward and outward man. The European appears to be one thing, but is really something else. He lives and moves in the falsehood of compromises. His entire culture is a collection of conventional lies to which he has adapted himself. He is extremely egocentric, but he conducts himself with absolute and almost exaggerated courtesy.

In the "underdeveloped" countries where the people still lack the finesse of European culture, everyone more or less expresses his inner world with some freedom and simplicity which you cannot find in Europe. Their manners are coarse, but the people are more genuine. In Europe this is considered a lack of culture and spiritual development.

In this way, the constant game of hypocrisy has come to be regarded as culture, where the white-washed tombs are full of stench, and the outside of the cup always cleaned for the sake of the appearance to the people.

But as it happens with Pharisees, that constant lie in which they live does not humble them. On the contrary, their outward perfection makes them certain of their superiority. The most characteristic mark of the Europeans is their conceit. They look down upon all the people whom they consider uncultured or underdeveloped.

A few of them might have a great concern for the needs of others, of persons, of groups, or even of nations, and especially the underdeveloped ones, towards whom they nurture compassionate sentiments, but deep down they are concerned for others the way an entomologist is concerned for insects. The sentiments they nurture for people are inferior to the love they have for their dogs.

They have the same high idea of their civilization as they have of themselves. Having critical minds, they do not accept anything unquestioned, and are proud of it. They consider all values relative, even those which they accept; and they discuss with apparent profundity all that humanity has ever believed.

Their customary position is that of well-disposed agnostics who are willing to agree with whatever you tell them, but let you understand that, of course, there is no way of proving anything you say, and therefore, it leaves them neither hot nor cold.

One thing, though, which these agnostics never think of doubting is the value of their own civilization. For them there never arose a higher civilization than their own. There might be sharp criticism about particular cultural problems and great disagreements over details, but the soundness of their culture's general direction has never been questioned.

The civilization of Europe is based upon a religion, but upon a religion which no one wishes to name as such, because this religion is not the worship of one or many gods, but the worship of man.

The religion of the ancient Greeks and their civilization was nothing else than the worship of man. If the civilization of ancient Greece found such a good reception in the hearts of Europeans, one can attribute it exactly to this inward kinship.

Like the ancient Greeks, the Europeans deified man's reason, his passions, the powers and weaknesses of his soul; in a word, they made man the center, measure, and purpose of all things. The culture of Europe proceeds from man; it exists for man; and it receives its justification from man.

There might be disagreements about the ways in which the improvement of man's life may be attained; there might be differences in the manner of worshipping man; there might be different conclusions drawn from man's measurement; but for all and always, man is the center around which they revolve, the source of their inspiration and purpose of their actions.

This is the European. Whatever religion he thinks he might have, deep down his religion is the worship of the idol "man." The European has ceased to see the image of God in man; he sees only the image of himself.

In other words, the religion of Europe is the old religion of humanity, the one which separated man from God. God's purpose is to deify man. But man, deceived by the devil, thought that he could become god without the grace of his Creator, on his own initiative and with only his own powers. He rushed to eat of the tree of knowledge before he was mature enough for such food.

The result was that his eyes were opened to know good and evil, to see his bodily and spiritual nakedness, and he was shocked. He could no longer bear to face his Lord and God, and he ran to hide from His face. He realized that a great chasm had been opened between him and his Creator. Then his merciful Father cursed the first cause of his destruction, the devil — "that old serpent" — and in His infinite love even promised salvation: "And I will put enmity between thee [the serpent] and the woman [the all-holy Virgin], and between thy seed and her seed [Christ]; and he shall bruise thy head, and thou shalt bruise his heel" (Gen. 3:15). And in order that man should not live eternally in that condition of spiritual death, He cast him out of Paradise, "that he should not extend his hand and take from the tree of life and eat and live unto the ages" (Gen. 3:22). Thus out of His compassion and love, God permitted bodily death and corruption, which, like spiritual death, was the result of the broken communion with the Source of life, so that man would not carry about through the ages his spiritual death, misfortune, and nakedness. And man, being separated from God and living in the constant reality of death, became a slave to the devil.

It was, therefore, as a reaction to the experience of his own nothingness that man worshipped man, proclaiming him god. In fact, the ancients taught that the human soul is a part of the divine nature, in other words, that it is divine in essence and therefore has no need of God.

This inward will of man to believe in his own divinity, together with the fact of his submission to the demonic powers, is the basis of every form of idolatry.

The religion of Europe, then, is none other than that primordial idolatry in modern form. Papacy, Protestantism, humanism, atheism, democracy, fascism, capitalism, communism, and anything else European, are expressions of the same humanistic spirit.

The civilization of Europe is nothing but the result of man's agonized and persistent effort to place his throne above the throne of God. It is nothing but the erection of a new tower of Babel; confusion about the method of erection may prevail, but the goal remains common for all concerned.

The ideal of the European is identical with the ideal of Lucifer. Deep down, it is the same contempt for the goodness of God, the same insult against His love, the same revolt and estrangement from His providence, the same ingratitude, the same desolate path which, instead of leading upward as man thinks he is going, leads to the abyss of death.

XVII. WITH THE CROSS AS BANNER

But the real religion of Europe is concealed and appears formally with a Christian mask.

For all the world, Europe is a Christian land. The devil is truly the clever one *par excellence,* and his jests have the most tragic consequences for humanity.

The greatest evil which ever befell the world had the Cross as a banner. The Aristotelianism of Western theologians and their discipleship to the idolatrous rationalistic thought of ancient Greece, the transformation of theology into philosophy, the adulteration of the Faith, the Papacy, the thirst for power and worldly authority, the Crusades, the mixing of religion with politics, the Inquisition, the missions which proved to be advance guards for colonizing powers, conquests, wars, the systematic blood-sucking of nations, orgies, frauds, humiliations, and tyranny took place in the name of the Crucified One.

In the face of this tragic deterioration of religion, it was natural that atheism and Protestantism should spring up as an aspiration for deliverance and health.

One should note that the atheism which appeared in Europe was not just an indifference, or agnosticism, or a simple epicurean disposition. The atheism of Europe was not an academic denial. It was a strong hate for the God of the Christians as they had come to know Him in Europe; it was a strong passion, a blasphemy, an indignation of the human soul.

In the Orthodox Christian East, from the time of Constantine the Great until the Greek Revolution, such epidemics never appeared. The people of the East had come to know a God completely different from the god which the people of the West had known; that is why they never came to deny Him, no matter how sinful they were. The first atheists in Greece came from Europe. Their denial, without their even knowing it, was against the religion which they had come to know in Europe. Their atheism was nourished by the faults of the Christians and the adulteration of the Christian truth which had taken place in the West.

Similarly, Protestantism might appear to be a separate heresy. But in actuality, it originated as a rejection of Catholicism. Protestantism never had a religious position. On the contrary, it was and is a religious denial. What justifies it is the presence of Catholicism. If Catholicism would disappear, then Protestantism would have no reason for existence.

XVIII. THE WAY OF KNOWLEDGE

Today, atheism as well as Protestantism might be turned against Orthodoxy. But this assault is based on a deception. They detest Orthodoxy because they see her with their own criteria, with their own mentality. They see her as a variant of Catholicism. This is not due to an ill disposition on their part, but to a total inability to judge by other standards and to think with another mentality.

Catholicism, Protestantism, and atheism are on the same level. They are offsprings of the same mentality. All three are philosophical systems, offsprings of rationalism, that is, of the notion that human reason is the foundation of certainty, the measure of truth, and the way of knowledge.

Orthodoxy is on a completely different level. The Orthodox have a different mentality. They regard philosophy as a dead end which never led man to certainty, truth, and knowledge. They respect human reason as no one else, and they never violate it. They regard it as one of the useful factors in detecting falsehood and uncovering error. But they do not accept it as capable of giving man certainty, of enlightening him to see the truth, or guiding him to knowledge.

Knowledge is the vision of God and of His creation in a heart purified by divine grace and the struggles and prayers of man. "Blessed are the pure in heart, for they shall see God."

Truth is not a series of definitions, but God Himself, Who appeared concretely in the person of Christ, Who said: "I am the Truth."

Certainty is not a matter of intellectual harmony; it is a deep assurance of the heart. It comes to man after inner vision and is accompanied by the warmth of divine grace. Intellectual harmony, which is the outcome of a logical ordering of things, is never accompanied by this assurance.

Philosophy is characterized by conceptualization. The human intellect cannot accept reality as it is. It transposes it first into symbols and then elaborates upon the symbols. But the symbols are counterfeit figures of reality. The concepts are as distant from reality as a picture of a fish from a live fish.

The truth of the philosopher is a series of figures and images. These symbols present one great advantage: they are comprehensible. They are cut to man's measurements and satisfy the intellect. But they also present a great disadvantage: they have no relation to living reality.

Living reality does not fit into the categories of the human intellect. It is a condition above reason. Philosophy is an attempt to transpose the suprarational into rational. But this is counterfeit and fraudulent. That is why Orthodoxy rejects philosophy and does not accept it as a way to knowledge.

The only way to knowledge is purity of heart. It alone permits the indwelling of the Holy Trinity in man. In this way alone is God and His whole creation known, without being conceptualized. He is known as He really is without becoming comprehensible and without being diminished in order to fit into the stifling limits of the human intellect. Thus the mind (*nous*) of man, living and uncomprehending, comes into union with the living and incomprehensible God. Knowledge is the living contact of man with the Creator and His creation, in mutual love.

The experience of knowledge is something which cannot be expressed in human words. When the Apostle Paul came to know, he said that he had heard unspeakable words—something which is impossible for man to express.

Such is the deeper Christian theology—inexpressible. Dogmas are helpful formulations. But they are not actual knowledge; they simply guide and protect from error. A man can have knowledge without knowing the dogmas, and he can know all the dogmas and accept them without having knowledge. This is why, beyond the affirmative theology of dogmas, the Fathers placed the deep mystery of negative theology where no definition is acceptable, where the mind is silent and ceases to move, where the heart opens its door to receive the Great Visitor "Who stands at the door and knocks," where the mind sees Him Who Is.

And let no one think that these things are true only in regard to the suprarational knowledge which is a movement of God towards man. Man can know nothing with his reason, and he can be certain of nothing — neither of himself, of the world, nor even of the most ordinary and common things.

Who honestly waited to hear Descartes' syllogism "I think, therefore I am" to be certain that he truly exists? And who waited for the philosophers to prove that the world around him is real in order to believe that it is? Besides, such a proof has never existed and will never exist, and they who are engaged in philosophy well know it. No one has ever been able to actually prove by his reason that our thoughts and our own selves, as well as the world around us, are not fantasies. But even if someone were to prove it logically, which is impossible, that logical proof would not be able to assure anyone.

If we are certain that we exist and that our friends are not figments of our imagination, this is not due to the proofs of the philosophers, but to an inward knowledge and an inward consciousness which gives us certainty of everything without syllogisms and proofs.

This is natural knowledge. It is the knowledge of the heart and not of the brain. It is the sure foundation for every thought. Reason can build upon it without fear of toppling. But without it, reason builds upon sand.

It is this natural knowledge which guides man in the way of the Gospel and enables him to separate truth from falsehood, good from evil. It is the first step which raises man to the throne of God. When man with his free will ascends the first steps of natural knowledge, then God Himself leans over and covers him with that heavenly knowledge of the mysteries "which are not permitted for man to utter."

The preaching of the Apostles and Fathers, the Prophets, and the Gospel, the words of Christ Himself, are directed to man's natural knowledge. This is the province of dogmas and affirmative theology. It is the manger where faith is born.

The beginning of faith is the heart's ability to grasp that the truth speaks in the small book called the Gospel, that in that commonplace church of poor and faithful people, God descends and dwells. When fear takes hold of one because he steps on the earth which the hand of God laid out, because he gazes at the great and broad sea, because he walks and breathes, then his eyes will begin to shed tears—tears of repentance, tears of love, tears of joy—and he will feel the first caresses of unspeakable mysteries.

Natural knowledge exists in all men, but it is not of the same purity in all. Love of pleasure has the power to darken it. The passions are like a fog, and that is why few men find the road to truth. How many people have been lost in the maze of philosophy, seeking a little light which they shall never see?

In this maze it is not important if one is a Christian or atheist, Protestant or Catholic, Platonist or Aristotelian. There is one common identifying mark on them all — darkness. Whoever enters the cave of rationalism ceases to see. And whatever garments he is wearing, they take on the same dark color. In their discussions they understand each other very well because they have the same presuppositions, the presuppositions of darkness. But it is impossible for them to understand those who are not in the maze and who see the light. And no matter what those on the outside tell them, they understand everything with their own presuppositions and cannot see in what way the others might be superior.

XIX. THE SCHOOL OF THE WEST

The debate which started centuries ago in the West takes place with amazing ease, and that is because the participants, although having different views, belong to the same school.

It is very difficult for Europeans, especially for Protestants, atheists, and the religiously indifferent, to realize how deeply their mentality has been marked by the seal of the Papacy and to understand that their negative views have been determined by the corresponding positions of the Papists.

The Papacy was the great pedagogue of the West. It taught the Europeans their first letters and initiated them into the rationalism which it had inherited from ancient Greece via Rome.

Rationalism was the soul of all heresies which warred against Christianity. All the theological battles of Christianity were fought against it. Heresy is the denial of the suprarational and the attempt to change it into something rational. It is the denial of the living reality and the acceptance of a concept, only because a concept is something comprehensible, whereas the living reality is not.

The Western Church began to be permeated with rationalism long before the schism. The Papacy and the various heresies which now embellish the "Church" of Rome had rationalism for a father. They were born and grew little by little through the centuries.

The remoteness of Rome and the difficulties in communications contributed to the fact that the first deviations were not detected in the beginning. Students of history will observe that for Christianity the West was always spiritually provincial. Nearly all of the spiritual and theological issues were born in the East, and their solutions were found there also. In the East the Christians were under constant spiritual tension. All the currents of heresy passed through there, and the spiritual battles took place there. The Westerners lived in a kind of bliss; they were the chocolate soldiers of Christianity.

The illnesses of the East were acute — the kind which create antibodies and immunity. However at the same time, in the West a chronic illness started — the kind that assuredly leads to death.

Rationalism brings with it self-conceit; self-conceit brings estrangement; and estrangement grows with worldly power. Thus, at the time when more than ever the West needed the spiritual assistance and guidance of the East, the chasm appeared, terrifying to the eyes of all.

In the meantime, in its effort to Christianize the peoples of Europe who were still barbarian, the Latin Church, instead of trying to raise them to the difficult heights of Christian Faith and life, tried to present Christianity as something easy and pleasurable, hoping in that way to bring the barbarians more quickly to Christ. Thus instead of raising the barbarian it lowered the Church. It made its teaching more comprehensible, more categorized, more systematic, more academic. In this way began the spread of rationalism and the adulteration of the Christian Faith. From a mystery and life in the Holy Spirit, Christianity became an ethical-philosophical system, which later found its best expression in the *Summa Theologica* of Thomas Aquinas.

Those who later rejected Catholicism received their culture from it. They grew up in it, and it had taught them how to think and philosophize. Protestants, humanists, atheists — the whole series of European philosophers — all graduated from the school of Catholicism. That is why they all speak the same language, the language of rationalism, and this is why, in spite of all their variances, they understand each other so famously.

XX. FEARFUL MYSTERIES

A discussion between atheism and Catholicism is possible. They speak on the same philosophical level, with arguments of the same order.

But a discussion between atheism and Orthodoxy is impossible, because Orthodoxy speaks a language which is completely incomprehensible to atheism. She understands atheism's language amazingly well, but if she speaks the same language, she will stop being Orthodox.

As an example, let us take the discussion concerning the nature of man.

Catholicism believes that man is composed of a body and a soul. Atheism does not accept the existence of the soul and teaches that man consists solely of the body. This denial was a response to Catholicism's view of man.

In an attempt to express the deep mystery of human nature in a simple form, the Catholics borrowed the Greek ideas about the soul and body, which were wonderfully comprehensible. They gave a definition of the body and a definition of the soul, which were both absolutely comprehensible. Like the ancients, they described the soul as an independent, self-existent entity, which man is primarily; they lowered the body to the level of an unnecessary burden which, as the Greeks believed, imprisons the soul and prevents it from developing freely.

In this way, the mystery of human existence fell to the naive level of a philosophical definition. That is where atheism found it and began to discourse about it, since atheism also moves on the level of philosophical definitions. Thus an endless exchange of philosophical-scientific arguments began, which will continue until the end of the world without proving anything, because the proof is sought in the sphere of pure reason and not in that which transcends it. Reason has only an auxiliary value; alone, it leads neither to knowledge nor certainty.

How could Orthodoxy, therefore, take part in such a childishly naive discussion without descending to the same level of naivete? Orthodoxy refuses to give philosophical definitions of what man is, what the body is, or the soul. She knows that man is more than what is apparent, but she also knows well that she can neither describe nor define the soul, nor is she able to regard the body or matter as something which is comprehensible to the human mind. As much as the human mind might analyze things, it can only comprehend the symbols which it creates itself, but not the essence.

Here is what St. Gregory of Nyssa says about man: "For as it seems to me, the make-up of man is awesome and inexplicable, portraying many hidden mysteries of God in itself."

Orthodoxy uses the words "soul," "flesh," "matter," "spirit," without always meaning the same things with the same words. She uses words which are taken from human vocabulary because she must express herself. But she never consents to enclosing within the narrow limitations of a human concept a whole mystery which even the angels cannot grasp. Neither does she consent to the dividing of man into air-tight compartments of body and soul, or, like some modern heretics, into body, soul, and spirit. Nor does she account little value to the flesh; rather, she often speaks of it as of the whole human nature: "And the Word became flesh."

But this is not our present theme. Orthodoxy is a spiritual experience, a life in God, a series of ontological contacts, and not a system of human syllogisms. Her syllogisms do exist, and they are most logical, but they are only aids. Her foundations are not of syllogisms and philosophical speculations, but living experiences of the divine energy in the pure hearts of the Saints. How, then, can atheism carry on a discussion with her?

XXI. THE LIGHT

Yet, there have been Orthodox in name who have entered into discussion with atheism and with philosophy generally. From various religious organizations of our land, scholars have been trying to prove for years that science also accepts the existence of God, but in spite of all their discussions, they have only managed to show how great is their own regard for science and philosophy and their ignorance of Orthodoxy. Being living examples of the Europeanization which we have undergone in our land [i.e., Greece], they did not wish nor were they capable of drawing strength from Orthodoxy to confound any and every philosophy. For all their theoretical Orthodoxy, they remain true Westerners.

The Orthodox has the power to prove logically to the philosophers that philosophy, if it wishes to remain rational, can only end in agnosticism, the denial of every knowledge. Every other claim it makes is unreasonable, and even though it appears to proceed from reason, it is founded upon imagination.

There is only one road to knowledge, the one which God has marked through the centuries. It is not a way of syllogisms but a way of life, because truth is not a system of philosophical theories but a personal existence: "I am the Way, the Truth, the Life."

But in order for one to walk this road, it is not sufficient to say and believe that one is a Christian. "Not everyone who says to me, 'Lord, Lord,' shall enter the Kingdom of Heaven." Something else is necessary: the lifelong struggle of the Christian, and that is purity of heart, which renders man worthy to receive the illumination of the Holy Spirit. All the moral and ascetical struggles of Christianity are aimed at this purity of the heart, with the purpose of the indwelling of the Holy Trinity in man. "Whoever loves Me, he will keep My word; and My Father will love him, and We will come unto him and make Our abode with him."

This direct communion with the Holy Trinity, this contact with divinity, the revelation of God, is knowledge. It alone enlightens man. It gives him to understand what God is and His creation. It enables man to penetrate into the reason of things and see what he himself is, beyond the phenomena and philosophical definitions.

In the face of this knowledge, what do the philosophers and atheists have to say? Will they deny it? They can. A blind man who has never seen light, of course, can deny that light exists. But this denial cannot carry any weight for anyone who does see.

One cannot prove the existence of light to the blind man. But if the blind man is well disposed, he will believe him and hasten to fall on his knees before Christ, beseeching Him to grant him eyesight. If he does not believe him, he will remain forever blind, and no one will ever be able to make him understand the greatness of his lack.

This is the relation of an Orthodox to the philosopher, the relation of one who sees to one who is blind. And just as it is not possible for the one with sight to carry on a discussion with the blind about the beauty of the earth, about colors and light, so is it impossible for the Orthodox to discuss the magnificence of knowledge with the philosopher.

Knowledge is something which you must taste in order to understand. No one can speak or understand what you tell him without the proper prerequisites.

Should, then, every dialogue of the Orthodox with the rationalists be cut off? Certainly not. The dialogue will continue as long as the blind and those who see live together. The blind will always talk as blind men. But the only thing is that those who see should not talk as blind men, since how then will the blind be made aware of their blindness? Those who see must continue to speak as men who see, even though it is not likely that they will be understood. At least in this way they shall be able to understand each other, and who knows, perhaps in hearing, some of the blind might come to see that without eyes one cannot come to know the light.

XXII. SALVATION

Many so-called Orthodox take great pleasure in participating in the discussions between Catholics and Protestants. And the blind would lead the blind.

For example, let us take the question of justification: that is, if it is faith or good works which save man.

The Catholics teach that man is saved by the number and the quality of good works he shall show at the end of his life. For a period of time the Popes even declared that the good works of the saints were much more than were necessary for their own salvation and that the merits which remained over could be disposed to the sinners if the latter could pay the appropriate price.

Rejecting the position of the Catholics, the Protestants taught that good works have no merit, that "man is not justified by works of the Law," and that faith alone saves man.

The debate has continued for centuries now with an uninterrupted exchange of an increasing number of arguments which convince no one, but turn around in the vicious circle of anthropocentric concepts which are so characteristic of rationalism.

What is the position of the "Orthodox" when they are confronted by this debate of the West? A feeling of inferiority and disorientation grips our theologians who stand ecstatic with admiration before the complexity of their Western colleagues' arguments. They do not know what to say. Inwardly they reproach Orthodoxy, which did not take a clear position in this problem. Some ally themselves with the Catholics with a few reservations; others try to reconcile the two views. The Apostles and Fathers do not help them at all; they seem to contradict each other and even themselves.

What darkness, truly, into which rationalism leads man! How can the rationalists understand the Apostles and Fathers, since the Apostles and Fathers, who were not rationalists, speak a language unknown to all rationalists?

For the rationalists, Holy Scripture, the simplest book in the world, is full of contradictions. For them every word and every expression has only one pre-defined meaning. Either the Apostle Paul is correct who teaches that justification is by faith or the Apostle James, who writes: "What is the profit, brethren, if a man say he hath faith, but has not works? Can faith save him? . . . Even the demons believe and tremble." That is why many Protestant theologians have characterized the Epistle of James as "chaff" and unworthy of being numbered among the books of the New Testament. But even the Apostle Paul seems to contradict himself in speaking one time about justification by faith and another about recompense "to each according to his works." That is why some Protestants have begun speaking of "two justifications."

The thought of the Apostles and Fathers is so clear, so simple, yet in the hands of rationalist theologians it has been filled with mist and darkness. They want Christianity to be a system. A system does not admit of antitheses. Everything must be in its place, properly classified. In their restricted thought, every antithesis is a contradiction. But reality is full of antitheses. Only when man accepts the antitheses as they are without trying to smooth them out does he approach the truth.

The Orthodox should glorify God because such a problem as this never arose in the Orthodox Church. The debate over justification which has continued for so many centuries in the West is void of any content. Salvation is not given as a reward for something good which man has accomplished, either faith or works. Salvation is not a reward, nor damnation a punishment. Such a concept, like all rationalistic concepts, is anthropocentric. It is a projection into the spiritual world of what happens in the daily life of men in society, where a good word or work is rewarded and a bad word or a bad work is punished by the laws which men have decreed.

Like the ancient Greeks, the West likewise made God according to the likeness of men. They see Him as a judge who judges and punishes on the basis of the existing laws. But the justice of God does not have a vindictive or legalistic significance. God does not punish to satisfy His own justice. Such a concept is out-and-out un-Christian. God never punishes anyone; He only chastises as a father chastises his son in order to raise him. Even Gehenna is not a place of torment but of self-exile, far from the presence of God. It is a condition of willful blindness, a place which never receives the rays of the sun. God is just, that is, good: for this reason He has no place or communion with the unjust, that is, the wicked. And this is not because God does not want to come near to the sinners, but because evil men turn away from the righteousness of God and do not want to have any communion with Him. "It is not He Who is hostile, but we; God is never hostile" (St. John Chrysostom, Homily XI on II Cor. 3).

Salvation, like knowledge, is a matter of communion with God. Works and faith, virtues and efforts are those things which open the door of our heart to the Lord. But that which gives salvation is not works, nor faith, nor virtues, nor efforts, nor all these together. A man might have all these and not enjoy the betrothal of the Spirit, not become an abode of the Holy Trinity. Salvation, like knowledge, is the vivifying of man by the grace of God and the vision of God, of which pure hearts are deemed worthy in this life according to the measure of their purity. It is not a reward forced from God by toils and labors, which might not have purified the heart at all, neither is it a reward for an intellectual faith, which might not have changed man's life at all.

XXIII. A GREAT CHASM

Catholicism, Protestantism, and atheism, like all other philosophies, speak the same language. One understands the arguments of the other, and in spite of all their controversies they can communicate with each other. But a great chasm separates Orthodoxy from all these systems, because it is something essentially different.

All the erroneous beliefs of the West and the drying up of its spirituality have rationalism as a basic cause. Europeans judge heavenly things with earthly standards and live their religion with the criteria and perspective of this life. One can cite such a multitude of examples that he could fill many books. But the two examples we have mentioned (i.e., the mystery of man and of salvation) are sufficient for one to realize that the difference between the Eastern Church and those of the West is not one of various characteristics, but a difference of essence.

Even if we were to presume that there was the best disposition on the part of the West to draw near and to live Orthodoxy — something which does not occur except, perhaps, in the case of the Old Catholics — this disposition would not render them able to understand and to live Orthodoxy. So many centuries of apostasy have not passed without leaving their seal on the souls of these people. And this seal is so indelible that it cannot be erased except by the grace of God, and then only from humble hearts.

In recent years, many in Europe have taken the name Orthodox and have been chrismated with the Chrism of the Orthodox Church, but very few of them have really become Orthodox. Most of them have embraced Orthodoxy intellectually, enchanted by the wealth of knowledge it offered them and fascinated by a new acquaintance with Christianity which bridged the gaps left in their minds by the mutilated Christianity of the West. But before they even received Communion for the first time and before they even shed a tear for their sins, before they sought the grace of Christ in silence and struggle, they considered it their imperative duty to preach Orthodoxy to the Orthodox. Scandalized by the ignorance of the Orthodox in theoretical matters in which they themselves shone, they scorned the Orthodox people who, although in ignorance, lived the Orthodoxy of their fathers and were ready to die for it. But God does not dwell in proud minds. Their theoretical preparation did not save them from error, and as blind leading the blind, they fell into the ditch of heresies leading others astray also, or they returned "as a dog to its own vomit" to their former worldly ways.

In order for one to understand the Saints and the Fathers of the Church, it is not sufficient merely to read them. The Saints spoke and wrote after having lived the mysteries of God. They personally experienced the mysteries. In order for one to understand them, he too must have progressed to a certain degree of initiation into the mysteries of God by personally tasting, smelling, and seeing. You can read the books of the Saints and become very well versed in them with a "cerebral" knowledge without even minutely tasting that which the Saints tasted who wrote these books through their personal experience. In order to understand the Saints essentially, not intellectually, you must have the proper experiences for all that they say; you must have tasted, at least in part, of the same things as they. You must have lived in the fervent environment of Orthodoxy; you must have grown in it. You must have tasted of training, effort, and struggle for Christian perfection. You must have bent very low to pass through the narrow door that leads to the Kingdom of Heaven. You must have been humbled; you must have been freed from the vain burden of human values and have detached the heart from that which men consider great and worthy of respect. You must have shed tears of repentance for the vanity in which you lived, tears of fervent supplication to the Lord to deliver you from darkness and to send down a ray of the Holy Spirit into your heart.

A whole new world must be born in a Westerner's heart in order for him to understand something of Orthodoxy. How can someone who has breathed the dry air of rationalism from the cradle and learned to worship human cleverness as an idol be humbled and become simple as a child? How can one who has learned to pursue those things esteemed "high by men" and "abominations before God" and has been taught to regard the turn to the inner man as "navel gazing" be saved from the thorns of worldly cares? How can he who has been taught to regard vanity as a value shed tears over the vanity of life?

What has Catholicism or Protestantism honestly done to protect the world from the relentless whirlpool into which it has fallen? But was it not the religion of the West that sent man running and panting to gain whatever Christ declared vain? Monasticism, the heart of religion, it either abolished or changed to utilitarian orders which either through their activity or through their thought had as their mission to serve the earthly well-being of men and the worldly wisdom which "God has made foolish." It made politics the province of Christian activity, swaying kingdoms and spilling blood in order to acquire power and money. It used missions as a decoy to subject colored peoples to the inhuman sovereignty of Europe. It pursued leisure and comfort, teaching that wealth is a gift of God. It gave Christianity a utilitarian, social purpose, causing men to believe that Christ was a moral teacher who is concerned above all with the orderly functioning of society, and the Church is the guardian *par excellence* of human laws and the overseer of law enforcement. It created the model for the pharisaic Christian, the good citizen, who thinks he has approached perfection because he has never harmed anyone, or because he has given money to philanthropic organizations.

How can men emerge humble, seeking the light from above with pain and tears, from a civilization ruled by the pursuit of human comfort and characterized by a satanic pride in the triumphs of its science?

How can a man who searches the depths of his heart to find in the silence and motionlessness of his "treasury" the "pearl of great price" emerge from a civilization which is characterized by unceasing motion and concern for externals?

Such a thing would be equal to a miracle of the rarest kind.

But if the savor of Orthodoxy is such a difficult thing for one individual, how is it possible for the entire Roman Catholic "Church" as a whole or all the Protestant "churches" together to savor her? Most of the millions of people of the West do not even know that Orthodoxy exists. How is it possible after one or more conferences of representatives of the various "churches" for a return to the truth to be accomplished collectively for souls walking in darkness for centuries now?

Do those who speak of the union of churches possibly think they are dealing with political affairs where the rulers of nations lead their subjects as a whole to either war or peace? People do not come to Christ and His Church in great masses. They come as free persons.

Let us suppose that a Pope suddenly decides to become Orthodox and to bring all the Catholics to Orthodoxy. With that outward change would even one of the millions of Catholics really become Orthodox? And even if they all had the best disposition to memorize and believe all the doctrines of Orthodoxy, they would not be able to take even one step towards her, because Orthodoxy is not only a system of doctrines or a series of customs, but something much deeper and substantial. It is a whole orientation of life and thought. Orthodoxy is a spirit, the spirit of Tradition, which cannot be acquired from books but is transmitted from the living to the living, from father to son, mother to daughter, brother to brother, friend to friend, priest to priest, monk to monk, from spiritual father to spiritual child, "not by means of ink and paper, but from mouth to mouth," from soul to soul. And all this within the life of the Holy Mysteries of the Church, within the atmosphere of the Holy Spirit, with the passing of time, little by little, with the slow development of an organism.

But those who speak of union are not naive. They know very well that the Catholics as well as the Protestants will never become Orthodox as a body. But that does not interest them. They are not interested in the return of lost sheep to the fold of Christ. They reckon on a compromise and are content with a superficial agreement. Besides, for some time now they have ceased being Orthodox. They are not concerned for truth or the life in Christ. Already the mystery of the Antichrist is working in them, and they are distressed until it be accomplished.

XXIV. THE FALLING AWAY

O unhappy Greek race! You who gave so many Fathers and so many Saints to the Church of Christ, you who enlightened so many barbarians and made them children of God, you who watered these rocks with tears of humility and contrition and made the garden of Orthodoxy blossom on them, you who brought God to walk on this soil through your prayers, why do you now turn your eyes ecstatically to where the sun never rose? And you who of old were God's servant, why do you fall upon your knees with servility to worship the servants of Lucifer?

Are you so overwhelmed by the signs and wonders of progress that you are ready to fall down and worship that glittering but empty idol? Do you not see the darkness behind the fireworks? Do you not see the despair of death behind the artificial smile? Do you not see the poverty hiding beneath the royal appearance?

What have you envied? The power of the Pope? But have you forgotten the power of your God which has enabled you to preserve your Faith intact to this day?

What have you desired? Knowledge? Yes, you should desire

knowledge, because you are beginning to lack it, lack it dangerously. But there where you seek it, knowledge does not exist; only substitutes for knowledge are found there — the academic philosophies and academic theologies. But these will only fill your stomach without nourishing you, for they do not have life in them; they are dead letters. They are the study of the shadow of things. They are not the study of God and His creation, but the study of the idea we have of God and His creation, the study of the concepts of our brain.

But if you desire an easy life, if Europe enchants you because it promises comfort and carnal pleasures, well then, go there. It will certainly give you that comfort and pleasure. But along with these, it will give you emptiness and death, the spiritual and eternal death it is tasting today.

XXV. THE SUMMIT OF THE TOWER

Let us not fool ourselves. The Greek race like all others will continue its way. And its way is the way of the masses. The way of the many is always the easiest. The way of the masses is always the way that leads to comfort and pleasure. And in spite of all we might say and all we might do, we would accomplish nothing because of the state the world has reached. The evil is irrevocable.

The most tragic thing is that evil appears to men's eyes as something good. The condemnation, which is not imposed by God but into which man falls by himself, will not be a destruction or some nuclear annihilation as people imagine. Actually the death of the body would be a very small evil for humanity. But that which is about to come will be something unimaginably more harsh and inhuman. It will be the masterpiece of diabolic imagination, the greatest hoax that ever has happened. The destruction towards which humanity is headed will have the appearance of its greatest success. It will be the summit of the tower of Babel, the peak of human vainglory, the crown of human self-conceit.

The destruction will be the fulfillment of the desires of the masses, in which every passion and every evil will swim about freely and unhindered. It will be a complete emptying of the heart, a void, a tedium, a boredom, in other words, spiritual and eternal death.

There will no longer be a place for God in the hearts of men. "In the abounding of iniquity, the love of the many shall grow cold"

(Mat. 24:12). The Source of life will no longer have a place among the great majority of people. The Gospel will have been preached to the whole of humanity, "unto a witness to men." All will know it, and almost all will have essentially rejected it.

In the luxury of the cities, amidst the creations of the human brain and the signs and wonders of the Antichrist, there will circulate human creatures without life, dead men who think they are living the most intense life that ever was, but who in truth will be biting with mania their own flesh.

XXVI. CIVILIZATION

They say the Pope is optimistic about the future of mankind. And he certainly should be! Humanity has become what for centuries he has been dreaming it to be. Let him marvel, therefore, at the work of his own hands.

All these learned, clever, and respectable people are his pupils. He first taught them arithmetic and letters. He introduced them to Aristotle. He taught them philosophy when they were still barbarians. To him they owe their civilization.

The Papacy did not preach Christianity. It had neither in appearance nor in thought anything in common with the fishermen of Galilee. The Papacy brought civilization to the Europeans. If anyone has the right to speak of a Greco-Christian civilization, it is the Papacy.

But what relation has Christianity to civilization? What relation can a religion which says "for here we have no abiding city, but seek the one to come" have with civilization, that is, with man's efforts to establish himself as comfortably as possible in the earthly city?

Yet if one carefully observes the sermons and pursuits of most "Christians," he will see that what they seek and hope for is not so much the glory of the Church as the glory of civilization.

Such "Christians" the world wants and accepts, because basically they have the same goals. But the others who do not speak of a Hellenic-Christian civilization but of monasticism, struggles, prayer, who have as their daily bread the continuous striving for the future city, these the world hates, for it does not recognize them as its own.

It characterizes the former as truly religious people, and the latter as overzealous, religious fanatics, deniers of life.

The kinship that exists between those Orthodox who speak of Greco-Christian civilization and the views of the Papists is astonishing. They have the same mentality, the same goals, the same indifference for the truth and the mystical life. Their "Christianity" is a cover, a world-view to fill the gaps in their mind and to make their earthly life even more comfortable.

Such "Christians" who are ever ready to make compromises in order to have the majority on their side will never disappear.

They too, like the Pope, are optimistic about the future of mankind, and they are justified. For both are struggling to build civilization, and civilization is being built and will be built better every day, to their great joy. It will be a civilization which will respect values, since a civilization without values is impossible, and the values are values because they are useful for society. But values will not prevent death from filling men's hearts. For values are sacrifices offered to the idol Man; they are not worship offered to God.

XXVII. THE DIFFICULT WAY

All that is written here is directed neither to the world nor to those "Christians." It is directed to the chosen few who themselves will be in danger of being deceived in the last times.

Within Christian organizations and within Papism and Protestantism, there are souls who truly desire God and seek the future city. But their environment and their teachers do not let them find the way which their hearts desire.

Those chosen few must be careful, very careful. The devil does not always act as devil; most of the time he appears as an angel of light. He preaches a Christianity just a little different from the real one, and with this trap many more are caught in his net than he would have gained by sending forth an entire army of atheists or Diocletians.

He stigmatizes the faithful, characterizing them as intolerant, narrow-minded, fanatics, letter-worshippers. In this way he has aroused against the Church of Christ the most frightful persecution ever. People are often more afraid of characterizations which diminish their honor and reputation than of the persecutor's sword. Very few are those who can accept the sacrifice of being considered stupid. But in today's world it is inevitable that every true Christian will be characterized as a fool, or at least narrow-minded. Very few have the courage to advance with such a prospect which approaches martyrdom. That is why most people prefer the easy way of compromises, and they preach it with fanaticism.

The pagan never hated the Christian as much as the "Christian" world does today. Formal tolerance is deceptive. The world tolerates only those so-called Christians who walk in step with it, those who try to apply a social Christianity and attempt to be always up-to-date. The others who do not agree to adulterate their Faith it hates. But the world's hate is a criterion for us to know if we are true Christians. "If they have hated Me, they shall hate you too."

CHAPTER THREE

XXVIII. ECCLESIOLOGY

The commotion about union of the churches makes evident the ignorance existing as much among the circles of the simple faithful as among the theologians as to what the Church is.

They understand the catholicity of the Church as a legal cohesion, as an interdependence regulated by some code. For them the Church is an organization with laws and regulations like the organizations of nations. Bishops, like civil servants, are distinguished as superiors and subordinates: patriarchs, archbishops, metropolitans, bishops. For them, one diocese is not something complete, but a piece of a larger whole: the autocephalous church or the patriarchate. But the autocephalous church, also, feels the need to belong to a higher head. When external factors of politics, history, or geography prevent this, a vague feeling of weak unity and even separation circulates through the autocephalous churches.

Such a concept of the Church leads directly to the Papacy. If the catholicity of the Church has this kind of meaning, then Orthodoxy is worthy of tears, because up to now she has not been able to discipline herself under a Pope.

But this is not the truth of the matter. The catholic Church which we confess in the Symbol (Creed) of our Faith is not called catholic because it includes all the Christians of the earth, but because within her everyone of the faithful finds all the grace and gift of God. The meaning of catholicity has nothing to do with a universal organization the way the Papists and those who are influenced by the Papist mentality understand it.

Of course, the Church is intended for and extended to the whole world independent of lands, nations, races, and tongues; and it is not an error for one to name her catholic because of this also. But just as humanity becomes an abstract idea, there is a danger of the same thing happening to the Church when we see her as an abstract, universal idea. In order for one to understand humanity well, it is enough for him to know only one man, since the nature of that man is common to all men of the world.

Similarly, in order to understand what the catholic Church of Christ is, it suffices to know well only one local church. And as among men, it is not submission to a hierarchy which unites them but their common nature, so the local churches are not united by the Pope and the Papal hierarchy but by their common nature.

A local Orthodox church regardless of her size or the number of the faithful is by herself alone, independently of all the others, catholic. And this is so because she lacks nothing of the grace and gift of God. All the local churches of the whole world together do not contain anything more in divine grace than that small church with few members.

She has her presbyters and bishop; she has the Holy Mysteries; she has the Body and Blood of Christ in the Holy Eucharist. Within her any worthy soul can taste of the Holy Spirit's presence. She has all the grace and truth. What is she lacking therefore in order to be catholic? She is the one flock, and the bishop is her shepherd, the image of Christ, the one Shepherd. She is the prefiguring on earth of the one flock with the one Shepherd, of the new Jerusalem. Within her, even in this life, pure hearts taste of the Kingdom of God, the betrothal of the Holy Spirit. Within her they find peace which "passeth all understanding," the peace which has no relation with the peace of men: "My peace I give unto you."

"Paul, called to be an Apostle of Jesus Christ . . . to the Church of God which is at Corinth . . . ." Yes, it really was the Church of God, even if it was at Corinth, at one concrete and limited place.

This is the catholic Church, something concrete in space, time, and persons. This concrete entity can occur repeatedly in space and in time without ceasing to remain essentially the same.

Her relations with the other local churches are not relations of legal and jurisdictional interdependence, but relations of love and grace. One local church is united with all the other local Orthodox churches of the world by the bond of identity. Just as one is the Church of God, the other is the Church of God also, as well as all the others. They are not divided by boundaries of nations nor the political goals of the countries in which they live. They are not even divided by the fact that one might be ignorant of the other's existence. It is the same Body of Christ which is partaken of by the Greeks, the Negroes of Uganda, the Eskimos of Alaska, and the Russians of Siberia. The same Blood of Christ circulates in their veins. The Holy Spirit enlightens their minds and leads them to the knowledge of the same truth.

There exist, of course, relations of interdependence between the local churches, and there are canons which govern them. This interdependence, though, is not a relation of legal necessity, but a bond of respect and love in complete freedom, the freedom of grace. And the canons are not laws of a code, but wise guides of centuries of experience.

The Church has no need of external bonds in order to be one. It is not a pope, or a patriarch, or an archbishop which unites the Church. The local church is something complete; it is not a piece of a larger whole.

Besides, the relations of the churches are relations of churches, and not relations which belong exclusively to their bishops. A bishop cannot be conceived of without a flock or independent of his flock. The Church is the bride of Christ. The Church is the body of Christ, not the bishop alone.

A bishop is called a patriarch when the church of which he is the shepherd is a patriarchate, and an archbishop when the church is an archdiocese. In other words, the respect and honor belongs to the local church, and by extension it is rendered to its bishop. The Church of Athens is the largest and, today, most important local church of Greece. For this reason the greatest respect belongs to her, and she deserves more honor than any other church of Greece. Her opinion has a great bearing, and her role in the solution of common problems is the most significant. That is why she is justly called an archdiocese. Consequently, the bishop of that church, because he represents such an important church is a person equally important and justly called an archbishop. He himself is nothing more than an ordinary bishop. In the orders of priesthood — the deacon, the presbyter, and the bishop — there is no degree higher than the office of the bishop. The titles metropolitan, archbishop, patriarch, or pope do not indicate a greater degree of ecclesiastical charism, because there is no greater sacramental grace than that which is given to the bishop. They only indicate a difference in prominence of the churches of which they are shepherds.

This prominence of one church in relation to the others is not something permanent. It depends upon internal and external circumstances. In studying the history of the Church, we see the primacy of prominence and respect passing from church to church in a natural succession. In Apostolic times, the Church of Jerusalem, without any dispute, had the primacy of authority and importance. She had known Christ; she had heard His words; she saw Him being crucified and arising; and upon her did the Holy Spirit first descend. All who were in a communion of faith and life with her were certain that they walked the road of Christ. This is why Paul, when charged that the Gospel which he taught was not the Gospel of Christ, hastened to explain it before the Church of Jerusalem, so that the agreement of that church might silence his enemies (Gal. 2:1-2).

Later, that primacy was taken by Rome, little by little. It was the capital of the Roman Empire. A multitude of tried Christians comprised that church. Two leading Apostles had lived and preached within its bounds. A multitude of Martyrs had dyed its soil with their blood. That is why her word was venerable, and her authority in the solution of common problems was prodigious. But it was the authority of the church and not of her bishop. When she was asked for her view in the solution of common problems, the bishop replied not in his own name as a Pope of today would do, but in the name of his church. In his epistle to the Corinthians, St. Clement of Rome begins this way: "The Church of God which is in Rome, to the Church of God which is in Corinth." He writes in an amicable and supplicatory manner in order to convey the witness and opinion of his church concerning whatever happened in the Church of Corinth. In his letter to the Church of Rome, St. Ignatius the God-bearer does not mention her bishop anywhere, although he writes as though he were addressing himself to the church which truly has primacy in the hierarchy of the churches of his time.

When St. Constantine transferred the capital of the Roman state to Byzantium, Rome began gradually to lose her old splendor. It became a provincial city. A new local church began to impose itself upon the consciousness of the Christian world: the Church of Constantinople. Rome tried jealously to preserve the splendor of the past, but because things were not conducive to it, it developed little by little its well-known Papal ecclesiology in order to secure theoretically that which circumstances would not offer. Thus it advanced from madness to madness, to the point where it declared that the Pope is infallible whenever he speaks on doctrine, even if because of sinfulness he does not have the enlightenment of sanctity the Fathers of the Church had.*

The Church of Constantinople played the most significant role throughout the long period of great heresies and of the Ecumenical Councils, and in her turn she gave her share of blood with the martyrdom of thousands of her children during the period of the Iconoclasts.

Besides these churches which at different times had the primacy of authority, there were others which held the second or third place. They were the various patriarchates, old or new, and other

---

* Actually, if we believe the Papists, we must either accept that all the Popes were saints and were enlightened because of their sanctity, or we must accept that God speaks through their mouth in a mechanical way, as He spoke through the mouth of Balaam's ass.

The first hypothesis is refuted when the life and works of most of the Popes who sat on the throne of Rome are examined.

The second hypothesis means that the mouth of a sinful Pope is moved by God and dogmatizes correctly, but he himself does not experience the truths that his mouth pronounces.

It is a basic truth of Christianity that God does not enter into communion with sin. He does not dwell in unclean hearts, and He does not enlighten proud intellects.

Sin is precisely the lack of light. It is darkness, the condition of men who wilfully remain in darkness because they "hate the light and neither come to the light." God, of course, could constrain them to come towards the light; He could make them saints by force, but His love towards His rational creatures does not permit Him to do violence to the freedom with which He has endowed them. Such a thing would be a refutation of Himself.

It is therefore equivalent to blasphemy for us to accept that God would forcibly enlighten the sinful Popes. If God had given the promise that the Popes would, in

important churches or metropolises. There exists, therefore, a hierarchy, but a hierarchy of churches and not of bishops. St. Irenaeus does not advise Christians to address themselves to important bishops in order to find the solution to their problem, but to the churches which have the oldest roots in the Apostles (*Adv. Haer.* III, 4, 1).

There are not, therefore, organizational, administrative, or legal bonds among the churches, but bonds of love and grace, the same bonds of love and grace which exist among the faithful of every church, clergy or lay. The relationship between presbyter and bishop is not a relationship of employee and employer, but a charismatic and sacramental relationship. The bishop is the one who gives the presbyter the grace of the priesthood. And the presbyter gives the layman the grace of the Holy Mysteries. The only thing which separates the bishop from the presbyter is the charism of ordination. The bishop excels in nothing else, even if he be the bishop of an important church and bears the title of patriarch or pope. "There is not much separating them [the presbyters] and the bishops. For they too are elevated for the teaching and protection of the Church . . . . They [the bishops] surpass them only in the power of ordination, and in this alone they exceed the presbyters" (Chrysostom, Hom. XI on I Tim.).

Bishops have no right to behave like rulers, not only towards

any case, teach His word correctly regardless of who they were, that would mean that He would speak with their mouth the way He spoke with the mouth of Balaam's ass. But just as the ass did not have any consciousness of what its mouth was saying, similarly, the sinful Pope would not have any consciousness of the truths which he was pronouncing.

You can give the entire Holy Scripture to an atheist to read. That atheist may be an able philologist and a theologian with a degree. But will he really understand anything from all that he has read? Give a miser the parable of the rich man and poor Lazarus, or an unjust man the Beatitudes to read, and then observe to see if they have understood anything from what they've read. As much will be understood by a sinful, proud, opportunist, and perhaps even an atheist Pope, of what God would put in his mouth.

But is that the way in which God promised to lead the Church to the fulness of truth? Do the Catholics believe such a thing? Let those who are not fanatical examine carefully how foreign such a mentality is to the Church of Christ, foreign to the thought and practice of the first centuries of the Church of Rome.

If they see this, perhaps they might not even need to search the Scriptures in order to find there the condemnation of every such teaching of Infallibility and of every form of Papism.

the other churches but also towards the presbyters or laymen of the church of which they are bishop. They have a responsibility to oversee in a paternal way, to counsel, to guide, to battle against falsehood, to adjure transgressors with love and strictness, to preside in love. But these responsibilities they share with the presbyters. And the presbyters in turn look upon the bishops as their fathers in the priesthood and render them the same love.

All things in the Church are governed by love. Any distinctions are charismatic distinctions. They are not distinctions of a legal nature but of a spiritual authority. And among the laymen there are charisms and charisms.

The unity of the Church, therefore, is not a matter of obedience to a higher authority. It is not a matter of submission of subordinates to superiors. External relations do not make unity, neither do the common decisions of councils, even of Ecumenical Councils. The unity of the Church is given by the communion in the Body and Blood of Christ, the communion with the Holy Trinity. It is a liturgical unity, a mystical unity.

The common decisions of an Ecumenical Council are not the foundation but the result of unity. Besides, the decisions of either an ecumenical or local council are valid only when they are accepted by the consciousness of the Church and are in accord with the Tradition.

The Papacy is the distortion *par excellence* of Church unity. It made that bond of love and freedom a bond of constraint and tyranny. The Papacy is unbelief in the power of God and confidence in the power of human systems.

But let no one think that the Papacy is something which exists only in the West. In recent times it has started to appear among the Orthodox too. A few novel titles are characteristic of this spirit, for example, "Archbishop of all Greece," "Archbishop of North and South America." Many times we hear people say of the Patriarch of Constantinople, the "leader of Orthodoxy," or we hear the Russians speaking of Moscow as the third Rome and its patriarch as holding the reins of the whole of Orthodoxy. In fact, many sharp rivalries have begun. All these are manifestations of the same worldly spirit, the same thirst for worldly power, and belong to the same tendencies which characterize the world today.

People cannot feel unity in multiplicity. Yet this is a deep mystery. Our weakness or inability to feel it originates from the condition of severance into which the human race has fallen. People have changed from persons into separated and hostile individuals, and it is impossible for them now to understand the deep unity of their nature. Man, however, is one and many; one in his nature, many in persons. This is the mystery of the Holy Trinity, and the mystery of the Church.

XXIX. PSEUDO-BISHOPS

It is imperative that Christians realize that the Church has sacramental and not administrative foundations; then they will not suffer that which has happened to the Westerners who followed the Pope in his errors because they thought that if they did not follow him, they would automatically be outside the Church.

Today the various patriarchates and archdioceses undergo great pressures from political powers which seek to direct the Orthodox according to their own interests. It is known that the Patriarchate of Moscow accepts the influence of Soviet politics. But the Patriarchate of Constantinople also accepts the influence of American politics. It was under this influence that the contact of the Ecumenical Patriarchate with the similarly American-influenced, Protestant, World Council of Churches was brought about, and its servile disposition toward the Pope started to take on dangerous dimensions and even to exert over-bearing pressure upon the other Orthodox churches.

America thinks that it will strengthen the Western faction against communism if, with these artificial conciliations, it unifies its spiritual forces. But in this way the Church becomes a toy of the political powers of the world, with unforeseeable consequences for Orthodoxy.

Are the Orthodox people obliged to follow such a servile patriarchate forever? The fact that this patriarchate for centuries held the primacy of importance and honor in the Christian world cannot justify those who will follow it to a unifying capitulation with heresy. Rome also once had the primacy of importance and honor in the Christian world, but that did not oblige Christians to follow it on the road of heresy. The communion with and respect for one church on the part of the other churches remains and continues only as long as that church remains in the Church, that is, as long as it lives and proceeds in spirit and truth. When a patriarchate ceases to be a church, admitting communion with heretics, then its recognition on the part of the other churches ceases also.

The Orthodox people must become conscious of the fact that they owe no obedience to a bishop, no matter how high a title he holds, when that bishop ceases being Orthodox and openly follows heretics with pretenses of union "on equal terms." On the contrary, they are obliged to depart from him and confess their Faith, because a bishop, even if he be patriarch or pope, ceases from being a bishop the moment he ceases being Orthodox. The bishop is a consecrated person, and even if he is openly sinful, respect and honor is due him until synodically censured. But if he becomes openly heretical or is in communion with heretics, then the Christians should not await any synodical decision, but should draw away from him immediately.

Here is what the canons of the Church say on this: ". . . So that if any presbyter or bishop or metropolitan dares to secede from communion with his own patriarch and does not mention his name as is ordered and appointed in the divine mystagogy, but before a synodical arraignment and his [the patriarch's] full condemnation, he creates a schism, the Holy Synod has decreed that this person be alienated from every priestly function, if only he be proven to have transgressed in this. These rules, therefore, have been sealed and ordered concerning those who on the pretext of some accusations against their own presidents stand apart, creating a schism and severing the unity of the Church. But as for those who on account of some heresy condemned by Holy Synods or Fathers sever themselves from communion with their president, that is, because he publicly preaches heresy and with bared head teaches it in the Church, such persons as these not only are not subject to canonical penalty for walling themselves off from communion with the so-called bishop before synodical clarification, but they shall be deemed worthy of due honor among the Orthodox. For not bishops, but false bishops and false teachers have they condemned, and they have not fragmented the Church's unity with schism, but from schisms and divisions have they earnestly sought to deliver the Church" (Canon XV of the so-called First and Second Council).

XXX. AT THE END OF TIME

The world and the devil are leading the Church to such frightening trials that the day might come when all the bishops of the land will enter into communion with the heretics. What will the faithful do then? What will the few do who have the heroism not to follow the masses, not to follow their kin, their neighbors, and their fellow citizens?

All the faithful will have to understand that the Church is not there where it appears to be. Liturgies will continue to be performed and the churches will be filled with people, but the Church will have no relation with those churches or those clergy and those faithful. The Church is where the truth is. The faithful are those who continue the unbroken Tradition of Orthodoxy, that work of the Holy Spirit. The real priests are those who think, live, and teach as the Fathers and the Saints of the Church did, or at least do not reject them in their teaching. Where that continuity of thought and life does not exist, it is a deception to speak of the Church, even if all the outward marks speak of it.

There will always be found a canonical priest, ordained by a canonical bishop, who will follow the Tradition. Around such priests will gather the small groups of the faithful who will remain until the last days. Each one of these small groups will be a local catholic Church of God. The faithful will find in them the entire fulness of the grace of God. They will have no need of administrative or other ties, for the communion that will exist among them will be the most perfect there can be. It will be communion in the Body and Blood of Christ, communion in the Holy Spirit. The golden links of the unalterable Orthodox Tradition will connect those churches among themselves as well as with the churches of the past, with the Church triumphant of heaven. In these small groups the One, Holy, Catholic, and Apostolic Church will be preserved intact.

Of course, it is wonderful that order and coordination should exist in the outward functionings of the various churches, and that the less important churches should receive their direction and guidance from the more important churches, the way it is now between dioceses, metropolises, archdioceses, and patriarchates. But in the last days, such outward relations and contacts will be impossible most of the time. There will be such confusion in the world that one church will not be able to be certain of the orthodoxy of another because of the multitude of false prophets who will fill the world and who will be saying, "Here is Christ," and "There is Christ." There might even be misunderstandings among the really Orthodox churches because of the confusion of tongues which exists in the contemporary Babel. But none of that will sever the essential unity of the Church.

A contemporary example of that condition is presented by the Russians of the dispersion who have been divided into three opposing factions. One group wishes to belong to the Patriarchate of Moscow. Another, in order to be free from Soviet political influence, belongs to the Patriarchate of Constantinople and is influenced by pro-Papal politics.* The third and most down-to-earth group, the Russian Synod Abroad, remains independent. And the three groups, at least up to the present, are Orthodox with full essential communion among them.** Formal intercommunion and external contacts, however, they do not have, and this because they have been lost in the web of legalistic concepts and debates about which patriarchate should govern them. Such a mentality is wrong in its very basis since there is no essential need for dependence on a patriarchate, particularly at a time when immense distance and frontiers of nations separate them from these patriarchates. Nothing impedes an Orthodox church in Paris, for example, from being in essential communion with the Patriarchate of Moscow or with the Church of Constantinople, even though it has no jurisdictional dependence upon them. The notion that the interruption of jurisdictional dependence of a local church from a patriarchate cuts this church off from the Orthodox Church is not Orthodox but Papal. Besides, even the existence of

---

* Since this book was written, this group has declared itself autonomous. Its counterpart in the United States is the Metropolia. (Editor's note)

** Of these three groups, two—the OCA and the Moscow Patriarchate—are now in full communion with one another, while the third, the Russian Church Abroad, is, at this printing, increasing its "unofficial" contacts with the other two groups. So long as each group professed the full Orthodox Faith in both word and life, they were true Orthodox Churches of Christ. However, since the author wrote the above in 1963, a number of decrees have been synodically enacted by both the Ecumenical Patriarchate and the Soviet Church, which place them outside the sphere of traditional Orthodoxy, i.e. (1) the mutual lifting of the Anathemas of 1054 on the part of the Ecumenical Patriarchate and the Papal see, and (2) the Soviet Church's decision to administer Holy Communion to Roman Catholics. Both of these acts contravene the commandment of love and the principle of

jurisdictional dependence of churches upon one patriarch is of Papal inspiration. An Orthodox patriarch is a president, a coordinator of efforts, an adviser of great importance, but he is not a despot, not a sovereign. He can do nothing beyond the bounds of his diocese without the agreement of all the other bishops (XXXIV Apostolic Canon).

It is possible, then, in the last days when the various churches and religions will have been united and will appear as a single whole, that the genuine Orthodox Church will appear disintegrated, fragmented into small, scattered, sparse parishes, so that it is even possible that one will suspect the other from lack of confidence, just as soldiers suspect each other when it is learned that the enemy is wearing the same uniform.

In the last days all will claim to be Orthodox Christians, and that Orthodoxy is as they understand it to be. But in spite of all this, those who have a pure heart and a mind enlightened by divine grace will recognize the Orthodox Church despite the apparent divisions and utter lack of external splendor. They will gather around the

faithful adherence to the truth which has been imparted to us by Our Saviour, the Apostles and the Fathers of the Church. Furthermore, the incorporation of two of the above-mentioned jurisdictions into the World Council of Churches as "organic members" belies their professed membership in the One, Holy, Catholic, and Apostolic Church. Orthodoxy in faith and life, and not jurisdictional dependence or adherence to a so-called "World Orthodoxy," is the criterion used to recognize an Orthodox Church.

In regard to the Ecumenical Patriarchate's 1965 "lifting" of the Anathema against the Papacy, that Anathema, in actuality, continues to be in force since the errors mentioned in the Anathema continue to exist within the papal church. Therefore, according to the 11th Canon of the Fifth Ecumenical Council, there was no "lifting" of the Anathema in 1965; instead, there was an *extension* of the Anathema, so that it now includes those who allegedly "lifted" it.

As for the Moscow Patriarchate, there was another development in September of 1986, when the *Journal of the Moscow Patriarchate* published a resolution taken by the Synod of the Moscow Patriarchate to "postpone" the decision to administer Holy Communion to Roman Catholics. But as the periodical *Orthodox Christian Witness* (Nov. 2/15, 1987) noted, "the only problem here from an Orthodox point of view is that one cannot 'postpone' giving communion to Roman Catholics. One simply *cannot*, under any conditions or at any time, give the Holy Mysteries to Roman Catholics, or anyone else who is outside of the Church." To do so would constitute, in the words of the OCA's Fr. Thomas Hopko (*The Orthodox Church*, April, 1987), a very grievous "sacrilege and blasphemy." Unfortunately, this "sacrilege and blasphemy" took place many times as many newspaper articles and photographs noted, and yet nothing was done or has been done to censure and correct those who were responsible. Aside from this, the Ecumenical Patriarchate's and the Moscow Patriarchate's joint prayers with the non-Orthodox continue and have now expanded to include even non-Christian religions, in defiance of all that our Saviour, the Apostles, Prophets, Church Fathers and Holy Councils have taught us. In what way, then, do these patriarchates represent Orthodoxy?

Hence, the continuance of the Soviet Church and other "official" local churches in the WCC clearly violate the precepts of the Holy Gospel and Holy Tradition. This continuing betrayal of the Faith "with bared head" places the Ecumenical Patriarchate, the Soviet Church and the other innovating jurisdictions in direct conflict with traditional Orthodoxy and with the anathema pronounced against the heresy of Ecumenism in 1983 during the tenure of Metropolitan Philaret of blessed memory. (Editor's note)

true priests, and they will become the pillars of the Church. Let the people of the world do whatever they will. Let there be ecumenical conferences; let the churches be united; let Christianity be adulterated; let the Tradition and life be changed; let the religions be united. The Church of Christ will remain unaltered, as Chrysostom says, because if even one of her pillars remains standing, the Church will not fall. "Nothing is stronger than the Church. She is higher than the heavens and broader than the earth. She never grows old; she always flourishes."

A pillar of the Church is every true believer who adheres to the Tradition of the Fathers in spite of all the frightful currents of the world which attempt to pull him away. Such pillars will exist until the end of the world, whatever might happen. Besides, when these things come to pass, the coming of the Lord will not be far off. That state of affairs will be the most fearful sign that His coming is approaching. Precisely then will the end come.

XXXI. THE SIGN OF THE COMING

Sugary, or unsalted and sentimental Christians regard the above as extreme and repulsive pessimism. As allies of the world, they cannot see the seal of the devil on that which they approve. Neither can they estimate the horrendous gulf which separates the world from God, for then they would be required to admit that the same gulf separates them too from God.

They cannot, therefore, tolerate anyone being pessimistic about the contemporary Babel. They are that content with their era. They see such a bright future. Christianity for them is very much in step with the world, and they are so pleased with this that they will never forgive you if you show them that they are deceived.

They visualize in the future a united world-church with all men united by the bond of love. The heretics of the various sects are to them their Christian brothers from whom they were separated by the egotisms and narrow-mindedness of bygone eras. They admit that there are dogmatical differences, but these differences shall be overcome by love, or to speak more openly, they shall be forgotten by love.

But what relation does that sniveling love have to the love of

God? How can they shamelessly claim that they have more love in their hearts than did the Saints who were not able with their love to overcome the barriers which divided them from heresy, but on the contrary, they made these barriers higher so they could protect the sheep from the wolves?

But that which they take for love of men is in its essence nothing but love of the world. It is a coming to terms with falsehood by men who cannot bear the hardships of the war with the powers of darkness.

And their dream, that idyllic image of good and kindly people who make Christ reign on this earth — that temptation of the desert — is a dream condemned by the Lord Himself.

Let the super-optimists cast a glance at the twenty-fourth chapter of the Gospel according to St. Matthew to see how the Lord prophesies concerning the last days.

And Jesus went out and departed from the temple, and His disciples came to show Him the buildings of the temple. And Jesus said unto them, "See ye not all these things? Verily I say unto you, there shall not be left here one stone upon another that shall not be thrown down."

And as He sat upon the Mount of Olives, the disciples came unto Him privately, saying, "Tell us, when shall these things be? And what shall be the sign of Thy coming and of the end of the world?" And Jesus answered and said unto them, "Take heed that no man deceive you. For many shall come in My name, saying, 'I am Christ,' and shall deceive many. And ye shall hear of wars and rumors of wars; see that ye be not troubled; for all these things must come to pass, but the end is not yet. For nation shall rise against nation, and kingdom against kingdom, and there shall be famines and pestilences and earthquakes in diverse places: all these are the beginnings of sorrows.

"Then shall they deliver you up to be afflicted, and shall kill you; and ye shall be hated by all nations for My name's sake. And then shall many be offended, and shall betray one another, and hate one another. And many false prophets shall rise and deceive many. And because iniquity shall abound, the love of many shall wax cold. But he that shall endure unto the end, the same shall be saved. And this gospel of the Kingdom shall be preached in all the world, for a witness

unto all nations; and then shall the end come.

"When ye therefore shall see the abomination of desolation, spoken of by Daniel the prophet, standing in the holy place (whoso readeth let him understand), then let them who be in Judea flee unto the mountains; let him who is on the housetop not come down to take anything out of his house; neither let him who is in the field return back to take his clothes. And woe unto them that are with child, and to them that give suck in those days! But pray ye that your flight be not in winter, neither on the sabbath day. For then shall be great tribulation, such as was not from the beginning of the world to this time, no, nor ever shall be. And except those days should be shortened, there should no flesh be saved; but for the elect's sake those days shall be shortened.

"Then if any man shall say unto you, 'Lo, here is Christ,' or 'There,' believe it not. For there shall arise false Christs and false prophets, and shall show great signs and wonders insomuch that, if it were possible, they would deceive the very elect. Behold, I have told you before. Wherefore if they shall say unto you, 'Behold he is in the desert,' go not forth; 'Behold, he is in the secret chambers,' believe it not. For as the lightning cometh out of the east, and shineth even unto the west, so shall also the coming of the Son of man be. For wheresoever the carcass is, there will the eagles be gathered together.

"Immediately after the tribulation of those days shall the sun be darkened, and the moon shall not give her light, and the stars shall fall from heaven, and the powers of the heavens shall be shaken; and then shall appear the sign of the Son of man in heaven, and then shall all the tribes of the earth mourn, and they shall see the Son of man coming in the clouds of heaven with power and great glory; and He shall send His angels with a great sound of a trumpet, and they shall gather together His elect from the four winds, from one end of heaven to the other.

"Now learn a parable of the fig tree; when his branch is yet tender and putteth forth leaves, ye know that summer is nigh. So likewise ye, when ye shall see all these things, know that it is near, even at the doors. Verily I say unto you, this generation shall not pass till all these things be fulfilled. Heaven and earth shall pass away, but my words shall not pass away.

"But of that day and hour knoweth no man, no, not the angels of

heaven, but My Father only. But as the days of Noe were, so shall also the coming of the Son of man be. For as in the days that were before the flood they were eating and drinking, marrying and giving in marriage, until the day that Noe entered into the ark, and knew not until the flood came and took them all away, so shall also the coming of the Son of man be. Then shall two be in the field; the one shall be taken and the other left. Two women shall be grinding at the mill; the one shall be taken and the other left. Therefore be ye also ready, for in such an hour as ye think not the Son of man cometh."

The disciples ask the Lord to tell them what will be the sign of His coming and the end of the world; and Christ, answering, begins with the words: "Take heed that no man deceive you." The danger of deception, then, shall be frightening in the last days; and that because "many shall come in My name, saying, 'I am Christ,' and shall deceive many." Many will come saying that they are Christ, or that they are His representatives or have been sent by Him, or are teachers of Christianity — people who will claim to be Christians without really being so. And they will not remain without evoking a response in men's hearts, but they will lead many into deception.

Christ, then, is not speaking of God's obvious enemies; He is not speaking of the materialists, of the communists, of the atheists, but of those who appear as friends of God, as Christians without being so in truth. It is from them that Christ wishes to save the faithful, because they are His great enemies, the hypocrites, "those able to deceive."

Then Christ describes a few signs which shall be the beginning of sorrows: wars and rumors of wars, famines, pestilences, earthquakes. All these shall not yet be the end, but the beginning of the end. "Then shall they deliver you up to be afflicted, and shall kill you," and the whole world shall hate you for My name's sake. Then many of the Christians shall be scandalized, and they shall begin to betray and hate one another. And many false prophets shall go among them and lead many astray. And as iniquity abounds, the love of many for God and for neighbor shall grow cold. The only one who shall be saved is he who shall bear all those temptations with patience and fortitude until the end.

In that chaos of apostasy and coldness, the preaching of the Gospel to the whole world shall be completed in order that all men may know it, in order that all men might hear the call of God. However, because "many are called, but few are chosen," people shall hear that Gospel, but they shall not accept it; they shall learn it, but they shall not live it. It shall remain "for a witness unto all nations," a fearful testimony that people know the truth, and that if they do not follow it, this cannot be attributed to ignorance but to an aversion for the light. Then "shall the end come." When these things come to pass and deliberate apostasy has reached its height, then the end of the world and the Second Coming of Christ shall come.

Then Christ begins talking about something outwardly unrelated to the end of the world: the destruction of Jerusalem. But that destruction which happened forty years later is in reality a prefiguring of the end of the world. When Israel's apostasy was complete, when they knew Christ and instead of accepting Him they crucified Him and persecuted His disciples, then the end of Jerusalem came. Then, as Daniel prophesied, the abomination of desolation came and stood in the holy place of the temple, and there was not left "one stone upon another," and everything holy and sacred of the Israelites was scattered and lost. The same thing shall happen to the new Israel, the Christian world. Just like the old Israel it too was called to become a child of God, but just like the old Israel it too spurned its benevolent Father, and instead of seeking the Kingdom of God it sought the kingdom of man. Therefore when its apostasy can progress no further, the prophecy of Daniel shall be fulfilled for it also. There shall be an abomination of desolation for it too, which shall stand in the holy place of God, in His Church and in His temples. The Antichrist shall come, who shall sit in the place of God and ask men to worship him instead of God. Then the sacred and holy things of the new Israel, the true Church of Christ, shall be scattered, hunted to the ends of the earth, and, as happened then when Jerusalem was destroyed by the Romans, as many as remained faithful to God and followed His Christ passed into the new Israel, so it shall happen at the end of the world, the true and eternal Israel, the true children of God, shall pass into the new Jerusalem, the city which is eternal and not made with human hands, and which the love of God has prepared.

Therefore, when you see the abomination of desolation standing in the holy place of God, let as many as are really faithful leave for the mountains; let them raise their minds to the peaks of the spiritual life; let them cut off their ties with the dead people of the world. Whoever has ascended to the high chambers of prayer, let him not descend from that heavenly conversation to the vain cares of this world; and he "who is in the field, who puts his hand to the plow," who does the works of God, let him not turn back to the vain works of men. But woe unto those souls which will still have the child in their belly and will not have borne any spiritual fruit, and woe unto as many as are still nourished on milk and have not tasted the solid food of the Spirit. Pray, therefore, that the end of the world may not find you under difficult conditions with your heart frozen and the feet of your spirit bound. For in that time great tribulation shall come to the faithful such as there never was from the beginning of the world. And if those days were not made short, no soul would be saved, but those days shall be shortened for the sake of the elect, so that they might not be deceived and lost.

Then if anyone tells you that Christ has come and that He is here or there, do not believe him, because there shall appear false Christs and false prophets who shall do signs and wonders in order to deceive, if they can, even the elect. And the Lord continues, "Behold, I have foretold it to you." So then, I have told you everything beforehand. If they tell you that Christ has come and is in some desert or some city, do not believe them; because when Christ comes He shall not come secretly, but His light shall appear to men like the light of a flash of lightning from east to west, and before Him shall be drawn up, against their will, all mankind.

Immediately after the tribulation which the faithful will suffer in those last days of the world, the sun and the moon shall be darkened, and the stars shall fall from the sky. And then the Cross shall appear in the heavens, "the sign of the Son of man," and then shall weep all the races of the earth, and they shall see the Son of man coming upon the clouds of heaven with power and great glory. And His angels shall gather up all the elect of God from the four corners of heaven and the earth.

When you see the fig tree bring forth leaves, you know from this sign that summer is coming. In the same way when you see all the things happening which I have foretold to you, you will know that the end is approaching. I speak truly in saying that before this generation of men passes, Jerusalem shall be destroyed, and before the generation of Christians passes away, before the evils which shall find them blot out their generation, all that I have told you shall happen. Heaven and earth shall pass away, but My words shall not pass away.

Do not ask Me which day or after how much time all these things will happen, for of that day not even the angels of heaven know. Only be always ready for that day, so that it will not come like a thief and find you unprepared. The days when the Son of man comes again shall be like the days of Noe. Just as in the days a little before the deluge men carefreely ate, drank, and married as though nothing were to happen, until the day when Noe entered the ark and the flood began which drowned them before they could understand what was happening, so shall the days be when the Son of man comes. At that time men shall be working together, and from them one shall be taken up near to God by the angels and the other shall be left far away from Him.

Remain, therefore, vigilant, because you do not know at what hour your Lord is coming.

XXXII. PERILOUS TIMES SHALL COME

Where, then, is the optimism for the last days? When the Lord foretells that deception shall cover the whole earth so that even the chosen shall be in danger of being deceived at their every step by the false Christians and false Christs who shall be everywhere, how can we be optimistic about the future? How can we be optimistic when the Lord foretells the multiplying of iniquity and the chilling of men's love?

Of course, there are forecasts of the union of churches, of the union of all those who come in His name to deceive many. But "take heed that no man deceive you; behold, I have foretold it to you." The union which the false Christians of our times seek is one of the most perfect machinations of falsehood, a snare of hypocritical piety from which the Lord wants to save us by making us cautious.

If the unity and worldwide expansion of Christianity is the final destiny of mankind as they teach, why then does Christ foretell tribulation for His elect in those days? If the Gospel will be accepted and lived by all the nations of the earth, why does Christ say that the days at the end of the world will be like the days of Noe, when apostasy had covered the earth, and only a handful of people were found faithful to God and entered the ark, which symbolizes the Church?

If the last days of the earth are characterized by the idyllic image of which the sentimental, the "spiritual" Christians dream, how does the Apostle Paul write these words to Timothy? "This know also, that in the last days perilous times shall come. For men shall be lovers of their own selves, covetous, boasters, proud, blasphemers, disobedient to parents, unthankful, unholy, without natural affection, truce-breakers, slanderers, incontinent, fierce, despisers of those that are good, traitors, heady, highminded, lovers of pleasures more than lovers of God, having a form of godliness but denying the power thereof" (II Tim. 3:1-5).

Where, then, is the optimism of the Apostle Paul when he writes to the Thessalonians, who were awaiting from minute to minute the coming of Christ? "Let no man deceive you by any means [that is, that Christ is coming right now], for except there come apostasy first and that man of sin [the Antichrist] be revealed, the son of perdition who opposeth and exalteth himself above all that is called God or that is worshipped, so that he as God sitteth in the temple of God, showing himself that he is God," Christ shall not come. "Remember ye not that when I was yet with you I told you these things?" And later he continues about the Antichrist: "And then shall the wicked one be revealed, whom the Lord shall consume with the breath of His mouth and shall destroy with the brightness of His coming, even him whose coming is according to the working of Satan with all power and signs and false wonders, and with all deception of unrighteousness in them that perish, because they received not the love of the truth that they might be saved. And for this cause God shall send them a working of delusion that they should believe a lie, so that they all may be judged who have believed not the truth, but had pleasure in unrighteousness" (II Thess. 2:3-5, 8-12).

The future then is not as beautiful as "they who perish" imagine, they who "receive not the love of the truth that they might be saved." It will be characterized by apostasy, the worst falling away the world has ever known. Because it will not be a clean and honest denial of God, but a hypocrisy, a falsification of the Faith and of the truth.

Did not the Fathers of the desert and the great cloud of Saints of our Church prophesy the same things about the last days? Here is a conversation between a disciple and his spiritual father taken from the *Evergetinos* (1958 edition, Vol. II, p. 114): *And the brother said to him, "What then? Shall the customs and Traditions of the Christians change, and shall there be no priests in the Church so that such things happen?" And the elder said, "In times such as those, the love of many shall grow cold, and there shall be not a little tribulation: overrunning of nations and movement of peoples, apostasy of kings, prodigality of priests, negligence of those in monastic life; and there shall be superiors disdaining their own salvation and that of their flock, all of them eager and outstanding at banquets, contentious, indolent in prayers, and eager to slander, ready to condemn the lives of the Elders and their sayings, neither imitating nor hearing them, but rather reviling them and saying, 'If we lived in those days, we too would have struggled.' And the bishops in those days shall be respecters of powerful persons, making decisions according to gifts, not defending the poor under judgement, oppressing widows, abusing orphans; and unbelief shall enter into the people, depravity, hatred, enmity, jealousy, rivalries, thievery, drunkenness." And the brother said, "What then is one to do in those times and years?" And the elder said, "Child, in such days as those, he who can save, let him save his own soul, and he shall be called great in the Kingdom of Heaven."*

From these prophecies which in great part have already been fulfilled, one can easily come to a conclusion about where mankind is headed. Its future is a spiritual bankruptcy, where love for God and neighbor will have grown cold, and men will have become to the extreme limit egotists, covetous, boasters, blasphemers, lovers of pleasure.

But that spiritual bankruptcy will not appear bare and monstrous as it is, but will be covered by an amazing appearance of religiosity. These people with their many spiritual ulcers will have none the less an appearance of piety. There will be many who will preach in the name of Christ and will deceive with their false piety and religiosity those "who perish," all those who do not have in their hearts the love of the truth in order to be able to discern the wolves in sheep's clothing. And furthermore, the false Christs and false prophets in the last days will accompany their message with signs and great wonders which they shall effect through the power of Satan (spiritualism, magic, fakirism, etc.).

Finally, when the faith of the great masses of humanity has been corroded by these false prophets and their souls have been prepared, then he whom the Jews awaited and still await will be revealed; it is he whose way mankind has been preparing now for centuries, he who will become the symbol and god of the entire lost generation of the last people, "the man of sin" — the great Satanic sin of the spirit — the son of perdition, the adversary, who like Lucifer exalts himself above everything which men have honored until then. He will sit in the temple of God as God, and by means of fearful powers and signs and wonders which he will perform with the power of Satan, he will prove to the darkened and shortsighted minds of men that he and no one else is God.

He will make the desired union of the sentimentalists a reality. Before his throne people of all the religions and spiritual currents will bow to worship as brothers. He will unite all the nations of the earth under his scepter because "power has been given to him over every race and people and tongue and nation. And all who dwell upon the earth shall worship him, whose names are not written in the book of life of the Lamb slain from the foundation of the world" (Rev. 13:7-8).

For worldly people, that preview of a universal state and universal religion is something very pleasant. It is the same today with those who desire the union of the churches and do not care about the truth. For the latter, dogmatical subjects are futile Byzantinologies. But "for this cause, God shall send them a working of delusion that they should believe a lie, so that they all may be judged who believed not the truth, but had pleasure in unrighteousness."

XXXIII. THE NEW JERUSALEM

In that society of the Antichrist, the few who will remain genuine

Orthodox Christians will be a rock of scandal, the only dissonance in all that diabolical harmony. For them, these days will be days of great tribulation:"And you shall be hated by all nations for My name's sake." It will be a new period of martyrdom, a martyrdom more of the soul than of the body. In that vast, universal state, the Orthodox Christians will be the outcasts of society. "And [he shall] cause that as many as would not worship the image of the beast should be killed. And he causeth all, both small and great, rich and poor, free and bond, to receive a mark on their right hand, or on their foreheads, and that no man might buy or sell save he that had the mark, or the name of the beast, or the number of his name" (Rev. 13:15-17). Yes, "then shall they deliver you up to be afflicted, and they shall kill you." "For the devil is come down unto you having great wrath, because he knoweth that he hath but a short time" (Rev. 12:12). "But he that shall endure unto the end, the same shall be saved." "But for the elect's sake, those days shall be shortened." Because "immediately after the tribulation of those days, the sun shall be darkened, and the moon shall not give her light, ... and the powers of the heavens shall be shaken, ... and they shall see the Son of man coming in the clouds of heaven with power and great glory."

Let the faithless mock, and let them pity us. The Christians do not live for this world. They have never accepted this world of exile as their fatherland, neither have they wished to adorn it as if they were to live in it forever. They live on this earth as refugees with a nostalgia, a nostalgia for the Paradise which they lost, a nostalgia for the fatherland. They may have been born on this earth, but the fatherland lives in their hearts, and in their every step they hear it calling them. They long for that moment, the moment of the trumpet, the moment when they will stand before the "serene eye" of their Lord, the moment when His gladsome countenance will face their countenance.

Christians are strangers in this world (St. Macarius the Egyptian). They are estranged, disdained, having a contrite heart and a sorrowful mind, living in a manner different from that of other people (St. Isaac the Syrian). They are as people holding their blood in their hands, not having confidence in themselves or thinking that they are something, but being despised and rejected more than all other men (St. Macarius the Egyptian).

You say that our religion is an opiate; you are correct. For you who have not experienced the presence of God, and whose heart has never leaped from the whisperings of divine grace, and whose eyes have never shed tears of divine love, for you who have never seen anything beyond the horizon of this earth, it is natural that our religion which denies the world should appear as an opiate. Truly, "if Christ be not risen, we are of all men most miserable." But Christ is risen, and every risen soul has lived this resurrection. It is natural for those who have not lived that resurrection to laugh at the Christians.

Many times Christians with irrefutable reason have shown the world how ridiculous are those who ridicule their Faith. But what of it? Did reason prevent them from believing? It is the mists from the mire in their hearts which do not permit them to see. Reason alone never enabled man to understand anything. So let them laugh. Their laughter brings faithful souls closer to the Lord.

We will allow you therefore to laugh. But what we will not allow you to do is to change the Gospel, to distort our religion and make it a servant of your own ends. We will never allow you to attribute worldly utility and expediency to our religion. "The Gospels do not speak of earthly things, but of heavenly things, teaching us a different life and polity, new riches and poverty, unprecedented freedom and bondage, another kind of life and death, a different world and order — not like Plato, who contrived that ridiculous *Republic* of his, nor like Zeno and the other politicians, philosophers, and lawmakers. For all of them had the following common attribute: they revealed that the evil spirit secretly inspired their souls. Our own conscience which protests proves that all their ideas were demonic devices, and all their teachings contrary to nature" (St. John Chrysostom, Homily I on the Gospel According to St. Matthew).

Christianity does not, therefore, prepare any earthly kingdom, any earthly city. It has nothing in common with civilizations and worldly systems. It has nothing in common with the caesars and the caesaro-papists. All the things which the people of the world pursue are on the level of corruptibility. The Christian thinks, lives, and moves in the world of incorruption.

Those who want to unite the so-called Christian churches do

not believe in the Church, do not believe in the religion of Christ. They simply use it. They use it for their own purposes. Their goal is the earthly city to which they wish to subjugate all men.

In reality, there is no question of union of the Christians. True Christians were, are, and always will be united. They were, are, and will be one flock with one Shepherd. Men, regardless of what name they have or to what religion they belong, have one destiny: to find the One, Holy, Catholic, and Apostolic Church of Christ, and to drink from the water "springing up unto everlasting life." The Church is one. People are many, and few of them are her children.

The city which is destined for the friends of God has nothing from this world. It is eternal, not made with hands, the existence of another earth, another world. "And I saw a new heaven and a new earth.... And I saw the holy city, new Jerusalem, coming down from God out of heaven. . . . And I heard a great voice out of heaven saying, 'Behold, God's tabernacle with men,* and He will dwell with them, and they shall be His people, and God Himself shall be with them, their God. And God shall wipe away all tears from their eyes, and there shall be no more death, neither sorrow, nor crying, neither shall there be any more pain, for the former things are passed away.' And He that sat upon the throne said, 'Behold, I make all things new. . . . I am the Alpha and the Omega, the beginning and the end. I will give unto him that is athirst of the fountain of the water of life freely.' . . . And they shall see His face; and His name shall be on their foreheads. And there shall be no night there; and they need no lamp, neither light of the sun, for the Lord God giveth them light, and they shall reign forever and ever" (Rev. 21, 22).

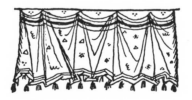

* The tabernacle in which God will live together with men.

REVISED APPENDIX

IS THE PAPACY A CHURCH?*

by

ALEXANDER KALOMIROS

> *"We have cut the Latins off from us for no other reason than that they are not only schismatics, but also heretics. For this reason it is wholly improper to unite with them."*
> — St. Mark Evgenicos of Ephesus

The Latins, who deep down are conscious of the lie in which they live, have felt of old the necessity to teach that their differences from the Orthodox Church are insignificant. This is but a means of quieting the struggling conscience of their faithful who continually uncover in Orthodox Tradition and life new magnitudes and depths which they lack.

They teach, therefore, that our only difference is insubordination, and that the dogmatic differences are only misunderstandings because of incomplete formulations. They fashioned the Unia, in which, without asking for any other immediate change in their faith and life, they accept Easterners if only they submit to the Pope. They believe that this peaceful assault is the best means of paralyzing our every resistance.

This cunning policy of theirs has diabolical psychological insight. They know that if they can convince their own people that nothing essential separates them from us, they keep them forever; and if

* This article first appeared in the June and July issues, 1965, of the newspaper "Typos," published in Athens, Greece, and was translated from it into English.

they succeed in convincing us that those things which separate us are unimportant, they have gained us also, for the feeble human soul always stands in awe before worldly power and great numbers, and it desires to have them as allies.

The victims of this propaganda of the Latins are for the most part ordained or lay theologians, who, having studied in a rationalistic, Westernized environment and having also the desire to succeed in a world of compromises which does not allow the absolute and the truth, have been disseminating for years now these self-same Papal ideas. With frequent repetition one can succeed eventually in making the most monstrous lie appear to be natural. Thus, most of our people who even up to yesterday, after an experience of centuries, regarded Westerners as the worst defilement of their religion and fatherland, today are in danger of becoming accustomed to the idea that the wolves in sheep's clothing of Papism are in reality unjustly treated by us and are misunderstood brothers in Christ.

Here is what our Papophiles maintain: "The Western Church," they say, "is not only a church in name but in reality, preserving in spite of the Schism and of dogmatic and other kinds of deviations the *charisma* of the priesthood and of the Mysteries."

They base this contention of theirs on the following arguments:

1) The Western Church has preserved the Apostolic succession in her ordination.

2) The Orthodox Church accepts the baptism of the Roman Church, since she does not rebaptize repentant Papists who come to her. This means, they say, that our Church recognizes the mysteries of the Papal Church and her ordination.

3) There does not exist, they say, a clear decision of an Orthodox Council which characterizes the Western Church as heretical and therefore alien to the One, Holy, Catholic, and Apostolic Church of Christ.

4) In the older official documents of patriarchs which were addressed to the Pope, the Western Church is called "Church," and this means that actually she is recognized

as being essentially in the Church by the patriarchs who wrote to her.

Let us see, therefore, how sound their arguments are, and what the actual position of the Orthodox Church is on this question, in order that the irresponsible opinions which have been abounding lately may cease.

Can it be that the Papists really have preserved Apostolic succession in their ordinations?

In speaking of Apostolic succession it is not sufficient that we prove a continuous and unbroken chain of ordinations which reaches to the Apostles. The Church of Christ does not hang from the letter of the law. If those who ordained did not have the right Faith, their ordination is invalid, and we can speak neither of Apostolic succession nor of priesthood. The laying of hands upon the ordinand by a true bishop transmits the grace of the All-holy Spirit. Does the Holy Spirit, however, abide where falsehood is? Where heresy is?

Here is what the Great Basil says, writing to Nikopolitas: "I will never number with the true priests of Christ him who was ordained and received the oversight of a flock from the profane hands of heretics, unto the overthrow of the Orthodox Faith."

The 68th Canon of the Holy Apostles states: "If any bishop, presbyter, or deacon accepts a second ordination from anyone, let both him and the one who ordained him be deposed; unless, indeed, it be established that he had his ordination from heretics. For those who have been baptized or ordained by such persons cannot possibly be either of the faithful or of the clergy."* Only if one has been ordained by heretics does the canon permit a second ordination, for the ordination of heretics is, in reality, as if it had never happened.

What value, then, does a merely ritualistic Apostolic succession have from whence the Holy Spirit has departed?

Their second argument to prove that the Papacy is a genuine Church is always cited by the Papophiles as the greatest proof of their theory. "Inasmuch as our Church," they say, "does not rebaptize Papists who desire to become Orthodox, this means that

* *Rudder*, **p. 119.**

their baptism and therefore their priesthood and their other mysteries are real and valid."

What great superficiality, however, is revealed by this conclusion! If this reasoning is true, then we must accept that neither the Arians nor the Macedonians were heretics, since the Church accepted for a time their baptism also. But away with such blasphemy! The baptism of heretics and schismatics is not Baptism. It holds the place of Baptism only when afterwards by economy the Church validates it. "One Lord, one Faith, one Baptism" teaches the Apostle Paul (Eph. 4:5). And the Council of Carthage, approved by the Sixth Ecumenical Council, explains: "For if the Catholic Church be one and the true Baptism be one, how can that of the heretics and schismatics be a true Baptism at a time when they are not in the Catholic Church but have been cut off from it by heresy? But if the baptism of heretics and schismatics be true and the Baptism of the Orthodox Catholic Church also be true, then there is not one Baptism as Paul proclaims, but two, which is most absurd."*

Also, St. Basil the Great in his canons does not accept the baptism of schismatics: "Nevertheless, it seemed best to the ancient authorities — those, I mean, who form the party of Cyprian and our own Firmilian—to class them all under one head, including Cathari and Encratites and Aquarians and Apotactites; because the beginning, true enough, of the separation resulted through a schism; however, those who seceded from the Church no longer had the grace of the Holy Spirit upon them, for the impartation thereof ceased when the continuity was interrupted. For although the ones who were the first to depart had been ordained by the Fathers and with the imposition of their hands they had obtained the gift of the Spirit, yet after breaking away they became common men and had no authority either to baptize or to ordain, nor could they impart the grace of the Holy Spirit to others, after they themselves had forfeited it. Wherefore they bade that those baptized by them should be regarded as being baptized by common men, and that when they came to join the Church, they should have to be repurified by the true Baptism of the Church" (Ist Canon of St. Basil).** Further on

* Ibid., p. 69.
** Ibid., pp. 773-774.

in the same text of St. Basil the thought of the Fathers is shown forth clearly, for they affirm that the baptism not only of heretics but even of schismatics is invalid—that is, without grace and sanctification. However, for reasons of economy they permit that it be confirmed afterwards upon the admittance of the schismatics into the Church. St. Basil, therefore, writes: "Inasmuch, however, as it has appeared reasonable to some of those in the regions of Asia that their baptism [i.e., of schismatics] be accepted as an economy to the many, let it be accepted."*

From the above, it is clearly obvious that the Fathers consider the baptism of heretics and schismatics to be non-existent. When they decide in certain circumstances not to repeat it, they are not, of course, changing their mind. They are making an act of economy in which the external and empty baptism of the schismatic or heretic obtains, upon his entrance into the Church, content: sanctifying power and grace which he, a man who until then had been outside of the Church, had never received.

If then, St. Basil the Great says such things for schismatics, "those who on account of ecclesiastical causes and remediable questions have developed a quarrel amongst themselves," as he defines them, let everyone consider how much more so these hold true for heretics, "who have broken entirely and have become alienated from the Faith itself" (Ist Canon of St. Basil),** and indeed for those heretics who are not burdened with only one heresy, but with a multitude of frightful and unnamable heresies, as are the Papists.

St. John Chrysostom also says: "Let not the systems of the heretics fool you, O hearer; for they have a baptism, but not enlightenment; and so they are baptized according to the body, but as for the soul, they are not enlightened" (Homily on "In the beginning was the Word"). And St. Leo: "No heretic confers sanctification through the mysteries" (Epistle to Nicetas). And St. Ambrose: "The baptism of the impious does not sanctify" (Concerning the Catechumens).

But, someone may yet wonder, if it be true that heretics do not have Baptism, then why did the Church in the Second and Sixth Ecumenical Councils accept the baptism of certain heretics such as the Arians and Macedonians?

* Ibid.
** Ibid.

Here is how St. Nicodemos of the Holy Mountain answers this problem: "In order to have an easily understood solution to this perplexity, it is necessary to know beforehand that two kinds of government and correction are observed in the Church. One kind is called 'Exactness' *(Akribeia)*, and the other kind is called 'Economy' and 'Condescension' *(Oikonomia* and *Synkatabasis)*. With these the Stewards *(Oikonomoi)* of the Spirit administer the salvation of souls, at times with one, at times with the other. So the Holy Apostles in their aforesaid canons, and all the Saints who have been mentioned, employed Exactness; and for this reason they reject the baptism of heretics completely; while, on the other hand, the two Ecumenical Councils employed Economy and accepted the baptism of Arians and of Macedonians and of others, but refused to recognize that of the Eunomians and of still others. . . . Those heretics whose baptism they accepted also rigorously observed the form and the matter of the Baptism of the Orthodox and were willing to be baptized in accordance with the form of the Catholic Church. Those heretics, on the other hand, whose baptism they had refused to recognize, had counterfeited the ceremony of Baptism and had corrupted the rite, or the mode of the kind, or (in the terminology of the Latins) species, and the same may be said of the invocations, or that of the matter, and the same may be said of the immersions and emersions, with reference to Roman Catholics and Protestants" (Second footnote to the 46th Canon of the 85 Apostolic Canons).*

We must well understand that when the Church for reasons of economy accepts the baptism of heretics or schismatics, it does not mean that she accepts that their baptism was a real one from the beginning. She merely accepts that the form of the baptism need not be repeated so long as the form resembled that of Orthodox Baptism. This form (triple immersion in the name of the Holy Trinity, etc.) does not sanctify the heretic except only at the moment when, repentant, he is accepted into the Orthodox Church by the Chrism. Then and only then, by the sanctifying grace of the Church, is value given to that baptismal form which that man had at some time received and which was till then a dead form.

We see, therefore, that even though our Church occasionally accepts repentant Papists without baptizing them, this practice does

* Ibid., pp. 70-73.

not mean at all that she accepts the priesthood of the Papal Church and its mysteries as being a true Church. We know very well, and all the Latins confess it, that our Church in the beginning always baptized repentant Papists. We have the witness of the Papal Council in the Lateran at Rome in 1215, which reports in its fourth canon that the Easterners would never liturgize where a Westerner had previously liturgized if they had not first blessed water there for purification, and that they would rebaptize those coming into the Eastern Church as if they had no Baptism. Therefore, if then, when the Papists had far fewer heresies, the Church rebaptized them, how much more so should it be done now when the Latins have added error upon error? "Therefore," writes St. Nicodemos of the Holy Mountain, "since until then, according to the witness of those self-same enemies [the Latins], the Easterners had been baptizing them, it is evident that for a great economy they used later the method of Chrismation . . . . So the need of economy having passed, exactness and the Apostolic Canons must have their place."*

"The baptism of the Latins," writes St. Nicodemos, "is one which is falsely called Baptism, and for this reason it is not acceptable either by reason of exactness or by reason of economy. It is not acceptable by reason of exactness for they are heretics." Further on he explains that neither by reason of economy is it permitted to be accepted, for the Latins do not even preserve the form of Baptism intact, inasmuch as "they do not perform the three immersions and emersions in accordance with the Apostolic Tradition. Therefore, the Latins are unbaptized," concludes the Saint. And further on—as if he lived in our days!—he adds: "I know what the unhired defenders of the Latin pseudo-baptism say. They argue that our Church became accustomed at times to accepting converts from the Latins with Chrism, and there is, in fact, some formulation to be found in which the terms are specified under which we will take them in. With regard to this, we simply and justly reply thus: It is enough that you admit that she received them with Chrism. Therefore, they are heretics. For why the Chrism if they were not heretics?"** The unhired (or hired) defenders of the Latin deception, says the Saint, gave it to be understood that since the Church became accustomed

* Ibid., p. 74.
** Ibid., pp. 72-73.

— 87 —

to accepting Latins with the Holy Chrism, without rebaptizing them, this signifies that she does not consider them as heretics and as completely alien to the Church. But, answers the Saint, to whom does the Church give the Chrism? Does she not give it to those who lack the Holy Spirit? Is not the Chrism "The Seal of the gift of the Holy Spirit"? Therefore, would she have ever chrismated them if she did not consider them as lacking the Holy Spirit, that is, as alien to the Church? The fact, therefore, that she chrismates them is the most manifest proof that she considers them heretics. Besides, it is Chrism, that gift of the Holy Spirit, which makes operative the previously dead Latin "baptism," and which the Church only permitted by economy not to be repeated.*

"That the Latins," he continues, "are heretics, there is no need of our producing any proof in this matter. The very fact that we have felt so much aversion for them for so many centuries is a plain proof that we loathe them as heretics, in the same way, that is to say, as we do Arians or Sabellians or the Spirit-defying Macedonians. If, however, anyone should like to apprehend their heresies from

---

* It should be noted here that the use of economy in receiving a non-Orthodox only through Chrismation without baptizing him was governed by whether the Orthodox form of triple immersion invoking the name of the Holy Trinity was preserved in the heretical baptism, not whether it was performed by a priest or not—for outside of the Church neither priesthood nor baptism is recognized. If the form of baptism were similar to the Orthodox form, then the Church through economy could give it content through Chrismation. Thus, for the Church the baptism of the Pope and of a Baptist minister are of equal status since neither have a valid priesthood. One can safely say that a Protestant baptism performed by triple immersion could more readily be sanctified by the Church through economy than the sprinkling of the Latins. It is evident that the present-day usage in certain quarters of receiving the Latins through Chrismation only is quite late and contrary to the Holy Apostolic and Synodical Canons and the mentality of the Fathers in relation to the usage of economy. The Church of Constantinople up until nearly modern times held firmly to the practice of baptizing repentant Latins when they were received. One of the accusations of Cardinal Humbert against the Orthodox in 1054 was, "That as Arians they rebaptize those baptized in the name of the Holy Trinity, and especially the Latins." The opinion of the great canonist Theodore Balsamon, in 1193, was that all not baptized through immersion should be rebaptized thus, including the Latins. In 1215, the same accusation as in 1054 against the Orthodox was made at the Fourth Lateran Council. In the first half of the fourteenth century, the great Matthew Blastaris holds the same opinion as Balsamon—that a baptism without triple immersion is no Baptism. In 1450, the Byzantine theologian Joseph Bryennios characterizes the Latins as unbaptized. Patriarch Jeremias II (1595) was of the same opinion, as was also Jeremias III, who in 1718 wrote to Peter the Great of Russia that the Latins were not to be received just by Chrismation. The Russian Church had already confirmed this opinion of the Church in the Synod of Moscow (1620) under Patriarch Philaret. But in 1666, at the Moscow Synod involving the Old Believers and Patriarch Nicon, the decision was changed; hence the letter of Jeremias III of Constantinople to Peter the Great.

books, he will find all of them in the writings of the most holy Patriarch of Jerusalem, Lord Dositheos, the Scourge of Popes, together with their most wise refutations. Nevertheless, one can also obtain sufficient information from the booklet of the wise Meniates entitled *A Rock of Scandal.* Enough was said concerning them by St. Mark of Ephesus in Florence (at the 25th Assembly), who boldly spoke thus: 'We have cut the Latins off from us for no other reason than that they are not only schismatics, but also heretics. For this reason it is wholly improper to unite with them.' And Sylvester, the Grand Ecclesiarch, said: 'The difference of the Latins is heresy, and as such did those before us hold it to be' (Section 9, Chapter 5). So, it being admitted that Latins are heretics of long standing, the immediate conclusion from this is that they are unbaptized, according to St. Basil the Great, cited above, and of the Saints preceding him, Cyprian and Firmilian. Because, having become common men as a result of their being cut off from the Orthodox Church, they no longer have with them the grace of the Holy Spirit with which Orthodox priests accomplish the Mysteries."*

We have seen, therefore, that according to the mind of the Fathers, schismatics and heretics have of themselves withdrawn from the life-creating and illuminating grace of the Holy Spirit, and so that which many call "Church" is in reality nothing but a dead body which, although it preserves the external marks of the Church, has lost its life. It would be stupid and blasphemous to consider that

In 1756, under Cyril V, the Tome of the Patriarchs of the East (see end of present article) was synodically proclaimed, by which the Latins were to be received, as unbaptized, through Baptism. A petition in 1750 by some Latins to be received into Orthodoxy at Galata became the cause of this Synodical Tome. In 1786, there was published a Canonical Decree by Patriarch Procopios which was sent to the former Bishop of Rashka (Rascia) Germanos, instructing him to receive the former Uniate Narcissus through "the one, true Baptism of the Orthodox Church." In 1803, Patriarch Callinicos published a second Canonical Decree upholding the one of 1786. In 1844, two Latin priests with their parishes asked to be received into the Church of Constantinople. The synodical decision under Germanos IV was that economy could not be used. Thus, they were all received through Baptism, including the two priests who were subsequently ordained. In 1875, it was synodically decided to permit by economy the reception of Latins through Chrismation alone. Three years later, in 1878, this was synodically revoked.

It is to be noted that economy can never take the place of Canons. The exactness of the Canons always holds and is to be returned to after it has been deemed wise at times by the Church to use economy. Till this day, on the Holy Mountain and in many parts of Greece, the Latins are baptized when they are received into the Church. (Editors' note)

* Ibid.

Papists, who are guilty of the worst schism that the history of the Church has ever known and of a whole system of heresies, have valid Mysteries and priesthood. The fact that the Orthodox Church of late does not rebaptize them when they repent and return to her does not signify, as we have seen, recognition of the mysteries of the Papal "Church" and its ordination, but signifies a conveying of life and grace to a dead form which would have remained forever a meaningless social rite if the person involved had not repented and been accepted by the real Church of Christ.

Is there any need for us to say any more in order to prove that the Papacy is nothing but a prodigious organization of heretics, without the truth, without Mysteries, without Divine Grace; that it is not a Church, but an organized worldly system with a religious veneer and, as other heresies, completely alien to the Church of Christ? But we shall continue and answer, with the help of God, the other two arguments of the unhired defenders of the Latin falsity.

The Latinophiles produce two other arguments in order to prove that the Papacy did not cease being a real Church. First, they say that inasmuch as Orthodoxy never convened a council in order to excommunicate the Papists, we have no right whatsoever to consider them as being cut off from the Church. Second, they maintain that since in the official correspondence with Rome various Patriarchs name the Papacy as the Western or Latin Church, or the Church of Rome, we must conclude that those Patriarchs consider the Latin heresy as being essentially a real Church.

Really, one is astounded with the willful blindness of these men! What truly happened in 1054? It is true that Orthodoxy did not excommunicate the Papacy. The haughty Papacy, however, excommunicated Orthodoxy. What more do the Papophiles want? What other official act could be stronger than that? What else could open a wider chasm between the Church and Papism? The Latins kicked the Church, but they kicked against goads. The theatrical scene with the Papal legates in the sanctuary of St. Sophia was the officialization, the confirmation, of the cutting off of the Latins from the Church of Christ. Is any other official act necessary? No one expelled Judas from the choir of the Twelve. He left by himself. No one excommunicated him. He excommunicated himself.

The Orthodox Church, say the Papophiles, never summoned a council to decide whether or not the Latins had been cut off from the Church. What nonsense! Which Orthodox ever doubted that the Papacy had been cut off from the Church? Whoever doubted it was not Orthodox. For after the official act of the Latin Church, there exist only two possibilities: Either the Papacy is really the Church of Christ, whereupon the Orthodox would be in reality anti-Orthodox and schismatics; or the Orthodox are the real Church, whereupon the Latins as heretics and schismatics have been cut off from the Church. What middle way and compromise is possible? The Church is one. Therefore, one of the two has ceased being the Church. Each Christian had nothing to do but to examine his conscience and choose. Whosoever remained Orthodox automatically renounced Papism.

Councils meet when questions and dissensions arise concerning a certain matter. However, in the entire history of the Orthodox Church from the Schism and after, there never arose a discussion or division of opinion concerning Papism. Even the participants in the false council of Florence were conscious that they had committed treachery. The Masses of the Latins were considered not only as empty of content but were considered as being a profanation—just as much as rites of black magic; and for this reason, as we have seen, when an Orthodox was to liturgize where a Latin had celebrated Mass, he first had a service of sanctification in order to cleanse the place. Not one repentant Latin was accepted by the Church without Baptism. Who at any time protested against these things in the Orthodox Church? But why should anyone protest? It was a common conviction of all that the Papacy was not a Church. Where then is found the need for summoning a council? What would the council discuss? Something which was already decided by existing conditions? Something about which not one Orthodox had, nor was it possible to have, a real doubt? The Latins were alien to the Orthodox Church, alien to its emotions, alien to its mentality, alien to its dogmas, alien to its religious life. How then could they consider them a Church? That would be tantamount to accepting that there was not *one* Church, as they confessed in the Symbol of the Faith, the Creed, but two!

Although no council was summoned to discuss whether the

Papacy is or is not a Church, nevertheless many councils were convened in order to discuss situations which every so often Papism created among the Orthodox. In the official documents and decisions of those councils, every man of good faith can clearly see what Orthodoxy believed concerning the Papacy. These documents settle things so well that they leave no margin of doubt even for the most disbelieving.

In the limited space of this article, however, only one official document is sufficient in order to fully demonstrate to the reader what the Orthodox Church has officially declared concerning Papism.

In 1583, the Pope of Rome, Gregory XIII, who changed the Julian calendar, repeatedly pressured the Patriarch of Constantinople, Jeremias II, who was called the Illustrious, to follow him in the calendar innovation. The Patriarch repeatedly refused with letters, and finally in the same year he convened a council in Constantinople at which, besides himself, were present the Patriarch of Alexandria, Sylvester, the Patriarch of Jerusalem, Sophronios, and many other bishops. This council issued a *Sigillion* which was sent to all the regional Orthodox churches and which enumerates the principal heresies of the Papacy and anathematizes (that is, proclaims as being out of the Church) all those who profess them. Here is the entire text of the *Sigillion:*

> To all the genuine Christian children of the Holy, Catholic, and Apostolic Church of Christ of the East in Trigovyst and in all places, be grace and peace and mercy from Almighty God.
>
> Not a little distress took possession of that Ark of old, when, storm-tossed, it was borne upon the waters; and if the Lord God, remembering Noe, had not in His good will calmed the water, there would have been no hope of salvation in it. In a like manner with the new Ark of our Church, the heretics have raised up a relentless war against us, and we have deemed it well to leave behind the present tome against them so that with the things written in it you may be able more surely to defend your Orthodoxy. But in order that the document may not be burdensome to simpler people, we have decided to set forth the entire subject to you in simple speech as follows:
>
> From old Rome have come certain persons who learned there to think like Latins; and the bad thing is that from being Byzantines (that is, Greeks) born and bred in our own parts, they not only have changed their faith, but they also battle the Orthodox and true dogmas of the Eastern Church which Christ Himself and the divine Apostles and the Holy Councils of the Holy Fathers delivered to us. Whereupon, having cut them off as rotten members, we order:
>
> I) Whosoever does not confess with heart and mouth that he is a child of the Eastern Church baptized in an Orthodox manner, and that the Holy

Spirit proceeds only from the Father, essentially and hypostatically, as Christ says in the Gospel, although He proceeds from Father and Son in time, let such a one be out of our Church and let him be anathematized.

II) Whosoever does not confess that in the Mystery of Holy Communion laymen should commune from two kinds both of the precious Body and Blood, but says that it is enough to receive only the Body, for the Blood is also there, even though Christ has spoken and has given each one separately, and they do not keep it, let such be anathematized.

III) Whosoever says that our Lord Jesus Christ at the Mystical Last Supper used unleavened bread as do the Hebrews and not leavened bread, that is, raised bread, let him be far from us and under the anathema as one who thinks like a Jew and as one who introduces the doctrines of Appollinarios and of the Armenians into our Church, on which account let him be anathematized a second time.

IV) Whosoever says that when our Christ and God comes to judge He does not come to judge the souls together with the bodies, but comes in order to decide only for the body, anathema to him.

V) Whosoever says that when they die the souls of the Christians who repented in this life but did not do their penance go to Purgatory — which is a Greek myth — where fire and torment purify them, and they think that there is no eternal torment, as did Origen, and, give cause by this to sin freely, let such a one have the anathema.

VI) Whosoever says that the Pope is head of the Church and not Christ, and that he has authority to admit into Paradise with his letters, and can forgive as many sins as will be committed by one who with money receives an indulgence from him, let such a one have the anathema.

VII) Whosoever does not follow the customs of the Church which the seven Holy Ecumenical Councils have decreed, and the Holy Pascha and calendar which they enacted well for us to follow, but wants to follow the newly-invented Paschalion [method of fixing the date of Pascha] and the new calendar of the atheist astronomers of the Pope; and, opposing them, wishes to overthrow and destroy the doctrines and customs of the Church which we have inherited from our Fathers, let any such have the anathema and let him be outside of the Church and the Assembly of the Faithful.

VIII) We exhort all pious and Orthodox Christians: remain in those things which you learned and in which you were born and bred, and when the times and circumstances call for it, shed your very blood in order both to keep the Faith given us by our Fathers and to keep your confession. Beware of such people and take care, that our Lord Jesus Christ help you. May the blessing of our humility be with you all. Amen.

The 1,583rd year from the birth of the God-man, Indiction 12, November 20th.

JEREMIAS, of Constantinople
SYLVESTER, of Alexandria
SOPHRONIOS, of Jerusalem
(and the rest of the Bishops of the Synod who were present)

This *Sigillion* is found in manuscript Codex 772, in the Sacred Monastery of St. Panteleimon, on the Holy Mountain, and manuscript Codex No. 285 of the cell "The Akathist Hymn" of the Sacred Skete of Kafsokalyvia, on the Holy Mountain. It was first published in 1881, in the periodical "The Roumanian Orthodox Church" in

Bucharest (12th issue), by the Russian Archimandrite Porphyrios Uspensky, who copied it from a manuscript codex of the great library of Mount Sinai.

Is a clearer or more eloquent condemnation of Papism needed than this one? Certainly not. Nonetheless, modern Greek "Christians" and "theologians" within themselves will scorn it, as they have scorned so many other Patristic declarations.

From all that has been written up to now, the answer to the fourth argument of the Papophiles naturally follows. Truly, in many official documents the Papacy is called the Latin or Western Church (although the attempt of the writers of these documents to use more frequently the words "the Westerners," "the Latins," and "the West," is obvious). It is, however, unforgiveable superficiality for one to attribute dogmatic content to such designations which are necessary for communication with people, since these names have prevailed in history, and they have not been abolished, among others, for reasons of politeness. Even the greatest warriors against the Papacy happened many times to call it the Western or Latin Church, although it is known that they regarded it as anything but a Church.

But if we finally accept that when a heresy officially is called a Church this signifies also a dogmatic recognition in it of the sanctifying power and grace of the One, Holy, Catholic, and Apostolic Church, then we must by all means accept that the so-called Protestant Church is a Church, inasmuch as it is called so officially. The same holds for the Church of the Seventh-Day Adventists, the Pentecostal Church, etc. But, then, if all heretics constitute the Church of Christ, to what purpose are the struggles for Orthodoxy? Then all the Fathers, Martyrs, and Confessors were the most miserable of men! Worst of all were those monks of the Holy Mountain Athos during the reigns of Michael Palaeologos and John Palaeologos, some twenty-six of whom were burned alive (at the Sacred Monastery of Zographou), others were butchered (Skete of Karyes), others were drowned in the sea (at the Sacred Monastery of Vatopedi and the Sacred Monastery of Iviron), others were hanged at Gallows Hill, and others were made captives and died as slaves from ill-treatment, solely because they did not want to accept the union with the Latins which the Emperor Michael Palaeologos had commanded together with a worthy predecessor of Athenagoras, the Patriarch Beccos.

Truly, for modern "Orthodox theologians" these Martyrs of the Faith were nothing but miserable, lamentable, fanatical, narrow-minded, and retarded beings, men who had not tasted the savor of love for our "brother" heretics, men who lived in the "night of yesterday," from which the partners and fellow-travelers of the "Cardinals of the Phanar" [the Greek section of Constantinople] are trying to lead us.

Let it be so, however. Christians were always "unto the Jews a stumbling-block, and unto the Greeks foolishness." This is their insignia and distinguishing mark. Such will they remain until the end, subjected to the persecution and mockery of the world. The world is nothing but a masquerade where everyone portrays a role, having his face covered. Many portray the good Christian, others the priest, others the bishop, others the patriarch, others the theologian, and others the preacher. All these the world tolerates with great ease because they are acting, because they too are masqueraders. Woe to him, however, who will dare to appear with an uncovered face. Woe to him who will not be masquerading, but will in all reality be a Christian, and especially woe to him when he begins calling everyone by their real name.

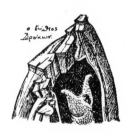

A FEW OF THE SACRED CANONS OF THE ORTHODOX CHURCH WHICH ARE RELATED TO THE FOREGOING ARTICLE*

10th Apostolic Canon

If any one shall pray, even in a private house, with an excommunicated person, let him also be excommunicated.

11th Apostolic Canon

If any clergyman shall join in prayer with a deposed clergyman, as if he were a clergyman, let him also be deposed.

45th Apostolic Canon

Let a bishop, presbyter, or deacon who has only prayed with heretics be excommunicated; but if he has permitted them to perform any clerical office, let him be deposed.

46th Apostolic Canon

We ordain that a bishop, or presbyter who has admitted the baptism or sacrifice of heretics be deposed. For what concord hath Christ with Beliar, or what part hath a believer with an infidel?

47th Apostolic Canon

Let a bishop or presbyter who shall baptize again one who has rightly received Baptism, or who shall not baptize one who has been polluted by the ungodly, be deposed, as despising the Cross and death of the Lord, and not making a distinction between the true priests and the false.

65th Apostolic Canon

If any clergyman or layman shall enter into a synagogue of the Jews or heretics to pray, let the former be deposed and let the latter be excommunicated.

* Epitomies of the Sacred Canons are given here. The complete text with notes and commentaries by St. Nicodemos may be found in *The Rudder*.

68th Apostolic Canon

If any bishop, presbyter, or deacon shall receive from anyone a second ordination, let both the ordained and the ordainer be deposed, unless indeed it be proved that he had his ordination from heretics; for those who have been baptized or ordained by such persons cannot be either of the faithful or of the clergy.

Canon I of the Regional Council of Carthage

That those baptized by heretics shall be rebaptized to be admitted to the Church.

Canon 32 of the Regional Council of Laodicaea

The blessings of heretics are curses.

Canon 34 of the Regional Council of Laodicaea

Whoso honors a heretical pseudo-martyr let him be anathema.

Canons 37, 38, 39 of the Regional Council of Laodicaea

Thou shalt not keep feasts with Hebrews or heretics nor receive festival offerings from them.

Canon 84 of the Sixth Ecumenical Council

Following the canonical institutions of the Fathers, we order that whoever does not know nor can prove by documents that he has been baptized, he must without any hesitation be baptized.

TOME

*of the Holy Church of Christ, upholding
the Holy Baptism given by God,
and condemning the variously performed
baptisms of the Heretics**

Of the many means that exist through which we are deemed worthy of our salvation and which are bound together in rising degrees, connected with each other inasmuch as they all look to the same end, the first is the Baptism delivered by God to the Sacred Apostles, which is such that without it all of the others are of no effect (for if one is not born, He said, by water and the Spirit, he cannot enter into the Kingdom of Heaven). It was proper and indeed necessary that there be created a birth different from the first birth which brings man into this mortal life, a more mystical manner — neither beginning from corruption nor ending in corruption — through which it might be possible for us to imitate the Author of our salvation, Jesus Christ. For the water in the font of Baptism takes the place of the womb, and that which is born from it becomes its child, as Chrysostom says. And the Spirit Who overshadows the water fulfills the function of God Who fashions the embryo. And just

---

*This tome is found in an interesting book entitled *Rantismou Stylitefsis* (Refutation of Sprinkling), printed in a second edition at Leipzig in 1758, in three languages— Greek, Latin, and Italian. The first edition came out a few years earlier in Greek at Constantinople under the saintly Patriarch Cyril V, who spent the last fourteen years of his life as a hermit at the Skete of St. Anne on the Holy Mountain. At the end of the second edition is an appendix in Greek of refutations of the Latin heresies by "our most holy Father Mark, Archbishop of Ephesus, the New Theologian," and a similar tract in Greek by Niketas Byzantios, "The Philosopher and Teacher." The whole work numbers 248 pages and is a rare edition. For those further interested, a Xerox copy, unbound, may be obtained from Holy Transfiguration Monastery, Boston, at cost (fifteen dollars).

as the Lord, after being placed in the grave, on the third day returned to life, so are the believers covered with water instead of earth,
imaging forth in themselves by the three immersions the grace of the
three-day Resurrection, the water having been sanctified by the
overshadowing of the All-holy Spirit, in order that the body may
be enlightened with the visible water and the soul may receive sanctification by the invisible Spirit. For as the water in the cauldron
partakes of the heat of the fire, so is the water in the font by the
energy of the Spirit transformed into divine power, purifying and
making worthy of adoption those who are baptized thus. But those
who are baptized in a different manner, instead of receiving purification and adoption, are shown forth as impure and as sons of
darkness.

For three years now, the question has arisen whether it is possible
to accept the baptism of heretics, which are performed contrary
to the Tradition of the Holy Apostles and Divine Fathers and contrary to the custom and prescription of the Catholic and Apostolic
Church, when they come to us. By divine mercy having been nurtured in the Orthodox Church and following the Canons of the Sacred
Apostles and Divine Fathers, knowing our Church alone to be the
One, Holy, Catholic and Apostolic Church, we accept her Mysteries
alone, and therefore only her Divine Baptism. But the mysteries of
the heretics, being inventions of corrupt men, are not performed as
the Holy Spirit ordered the Sacred Apostles and as the Church of
Christ until today performs. Thus, knowing them to be strange and
foreign to the entire Apostolic Tradition, we abhor them by common decision. Those, therefore, of them who come unto us, we receive as profane and unbaptized, following both our Lord Jesus
Christ Who commanded His disciples, "Baptize in the name of the
Father, and of the Son, and of the Holy Spirit," and the Sacred
and Divine Apostles who ordered that those who drew near are to
be baptized with three immersions and emersions, with each immersion invoking one name of the Holy Trinity. Also, following
the Sacred and Equal-to-the-Apostles Dionysios, who says, "He
who comes unto us, after having all clothing removed, is immersed
thrice in the font containing water and sanctified oil, invoking the
threefold hypostases of the Divine Blessedness, and immediately
the baptized is sealed with the Divinely-working Myrrh and is shown

forth therefore as a participant in the sacredly performed Eucharist." Following also both the Second and Fifth-Sixth (Quinsext) Holy Ecumenical Councils which order that they who were not baptized with three immersions and emersions, or at each immersion no invocation of one of the Divine Hypostases was exclaimed, but were baptized differently, are to be considered as unbaptized when they come to Orthodoxy.

We, therefore, following these Sacred and Divine Precepts, hold that the baptisms of the heretics, since they are not in accord with and are foreign to the Divine Apostolic Decree, being useless waters, as the Sacred Ambrose and the Great Athanasius say, granting no sanctification to those who receive them and profiting not at all for the purification from sins, are to be rejected and avoided as an abomination. And those who come to the Orthodox Faith with false baptism, we receive as unbaptized, and with no danger we baptize them according to both the Apostolic and Synodical Canons, upon which the Holy, Catholic, and Apostolic Church of Christ, the common Mother of us all, is firmly built up.

And with this our common resolution and decision, we seal this our Tome, which is in harmony with the Apostolic and Synodical Decrees, confirming it by our signatures.*

In the Year of Salvation, 1756

CYRIL, by the mercy of God, Archbishop of Constantinople
(New Rome) and Ecumenical Patriarch.

MATTHEW, by the mercy of God, Pope and Patriarch of the
Great City of Alexandria and Judge of the Ecumene.

PARTHENIOS, by the mercy of God, Patriarch of the Holy City
Jerusalem and all Palestine.

---

* The Patriarch of Antioch, Sylvester, was not present at the Synod, but was also in agreement with the declaration and expressed his approval.

Many prominent churchmen of the time were consulted, and the consensus of opinion was to adhere strictly to the Canons whereby the Orthodox Baptism alone was recognized as valid.

PROCLAMATION*

of the Holy Mountain, Athos,
to the pious Orthodox Greek people and
the whole of the Orthodox Church

The undersigned Fathers of the Holy Mountain, abbots, priest-monks, and monks, learning of the recent machinations and plots against our blameless Orthodox Faith by the Papal insurrection and of the pro-uniate actions and statements of the Ecumenical Patriarch and his co-workers, do proclaim with a stentorian voice that we denounce these uniate tendencies and leanings, and remain steadfast and unshaken in our Orthodox Faith, following all that the godly Prophets prophesied, and the God-proclaiming Apostles, the Assembly of the God-bearing Fathers, the Seven Holy Ecumenical Councils and other Regional Councils taught, having as Head the Chief Cornerstone, Christ our God, and in general adhere to all which our Orthodox Faith teaches either by script or by Holy Tradition, rejecting "Union" or "Unity" which the pro-uniates propagate of late.

If the Roman Catholics and other heretics wish to return to Orthodoxy, they are free to come and seek the mercy of God, em-

* The present proclamation of the Holy Mountain, Athos, was drawn up immediately after Patriarch Athenagoras met and prayed with Pope Paul in Jerusalem, and was first published in "Agioritiki Bibliotheki," May-June issue, 1964, pp. 161-164. At that time the Monastery of Simonopetra immediately ceased commemorating the Patriarch at the Divine Liturgy. Since then, there have followed many letters, articles, and appeals written by various abbots and monks to the Patriarch, calling upon him to make a clear statement of Faith and to cease from his scandalous statements and actions. The "answer" was the lifting of the Anathemas of 1054 in December, 1965. Thus, today with the exception of a few, all monasteries of the Holy Mountain and all the sketes and hermitages have followed the example of Simonopetra and have ceased commemorating Patriarch Athenagoras in the Divine Liturgy, as having apostatized and fallen under the ban of the numerous canons which he has broken.

bracing in its entirety the dogmas and Traditions of our blameless Orthodox Faith. It is by no means expedient that we Orthodox should run to them at the expense of Truth. We make an appeal to the Ecumenical Patriarch to cease from following his pro-uniate activities, for if he persists we shall disavow him also. We declare beforehand that we shall contend unto our last breath for our Orthodoxy, even shedding our blood if the occasion demands it, imitating our ever-memorable predecessors and crying out with the blessed Joseph Bryennios: "We shall never renounce thee, beloved Orthodoxy! We shall never betray thee, O Reverence of the Fathers! We shall never abandon thee, Mother Piety! In thee were we born; in thee do we live; and in thee shall we repose. And if the times demand, we shall die a thousand times for you."

We laud the Venerable Archbishop of the Orthodox Church of Greece and the whole Orthodox Hierarchy of Greece for their strong stand on behalf of Orthodoxy, and we make it known that we stand by their side.

On the Holy Mountain, the 23rd of January, 1964 (Old Calendar).

The Abbot of Dionysiou, Archimandrite Gabriel, and the brethren in Christ with me.

The Abbot of the Sacred Cenobion of Grigoriou, Archim. Bessarion, and the brethren in Christ with me.

The Abbot of the Sacred Monastery of Simonopetra, Archim. Haralampos.

The Abbot of the Sacred Monastery of Xenophon, Archim. Eudokimos, and the brethren in Christ with me.

The Epitropoi of the Sacred Monastery of Iviron, Elder Agathangelos, Proegoumenos Methodios, Elder Gervasios, Athanasios, Ivirite priestmonk, and all our brotherhood in Christ.

Theoklitos, monk Dionysiates, Hesychasterion of St. Gerasimos.

Gabriel, priestmonk and confessor
Elder Gelasios of Simonopetra
Elder Hesychios, priestmonk of Simonopetra
Elder Neophytos, priestmonk of Simonopetra
The Dikaios of the Sacred Skete of Iviron, Priestmonk

Neilos, and the brethren in Christ with me.

Proegoumenos Kosmas of Philotheou, First Epitropos.

Proegoumenos Eumenios of Philotheou signs with his whole heart.

The Secretary of the Sacred Monastery Karakalou, Elder Euthymios, Proistamenos.

The holy hesychast Fathers in Provata.

The Priestmonk of the Russian Kelli of the Precious Cross, Metrophanes.

Sacred Deacon Demetrios and synodia.

Neophytos, priestmonk Agiannanite, and those with me.

Matthias, monk, Skete of the Honorable Forerunner.

Achilleios, monk, Kelli of the Presentation

Hesychios, priestmonk, Skete of St. Anne

Ananias, priestmonk Agiannanite

Anthony, monk Agiannanite; Cyril, monk

Constantios, priestmonk Agiannanite

John, Averkios, Chrysostom, monks

Symeon, monk; Andreas, monk Agiannanite

Seraphim Papademetriou, priestmonk Agiannanite

Sabbas, monk Agiannanite; Dionysios, monk

Euthymios, monk; Anthony, monk, Kelli of St. Anthony

Cosmas, monk; Chrysostom, monk

Neophytos the tailor, priestmonk

Seraphim Kartsones, priestmonk, and the brethren with me.

Clement, monk; Nestor, monk

Anthimos Zapheiropoulos, priestmonk, and the brethren with me.

Haralampos, monk, and the brethren with me.

Ephraim, priestmonk; Dionysios, monk

Euthymios, monk; Gregory, monk

Ioasaph, monk; Alexios, monk

John, monk; Nectarios, monk; Gerontios, monk,

Athanasios and Cyril, monks Agiannanites

Philip, monk, and Nicander, monk, Agiannanites

Modestos, monk Agiannanite

Panaretos, monk Xenophonite

Euthymios, monk; priestmonk Matthew

Nicodemos, monk; John, monk, Kelli of St. Panteleimon

NEW SKETE

The Dikaios, Cyril, monk
Constantine Mourtos, monk
Athanasios, monk of Joseph; Menas Zacharas, monk
Theodosios, monk and synodia; Anthony, monk
Priestmonk Seraphim; Andreas, monk
Abramios, monk; Paul, monk; Luke, monk
Thomas, sacred deacon; Silvester, monk
Dorotheos and Procopios; Hesychios, monk
Mark, monk; Stephen, monk; Chrysostom, monk
Eustratios, monk, Hut of the Honorable Forerunner
Hesychasts: Arsenios; monk of Joseph, Priestmonk Haralampos,
Joseph the Cave-dweller, hermit; Priestmonk Ephraim* with my
synodia in Christ.
Nicholas, Chrysostom, monks; Callistos, monk
Theophylactos, monk; Ananias, monk
Damascene, monk; Elder Parthenios; Sabbas, monk
Chrysanthos, priestmonk; Niphon, monk; Kallistratos, monk
Elder Gerasimos Papacyril, monk; Macarios, monk
lgnatios, monk; Athanasios Papacyril, monk
Athanasios Broules, monk; Tryphon, monk
Sabbas, monk; Modestos, monk Agiopetrite.

SACRED SKETE OF THE HOLY TRINITY, KAFSOKALYVIA

Joachim, monk, and synodia
Proegumenos Damian and synodia
Michael, monk, and synodia; Gabriel, monk
Daniel, monk, with my synodia
Eudokimos, monk, Hut of St. loasaph, with all my heart
Panteleimon, monk
John, monk; Anthony, monk; Anthony, monk, Hut of St.
John the Theologian, with the synodia.
Basil, monk, Kelli of the Entrance
Luke, monk, Kelli of the Holy Apostles

*This is the same Elder Ephraim who is now under the Ecumenical Patriarch, and has
established numerous monasteries & convents in North Amercia.

Eugenios, monk
Stephen, monk
Michael, monk
Symeon and his synodia
Hierotheos, monk
Priestmonk Nicodemos, Paisius, monk; Anthimos, monk
Anthony, monk, Hut of the Righteous Fathers
Esaias, monk
Elder Isidore, monk. and synodia
Seraphim, monk
Haralampos, monk
Cosmas Stavroudas, monk
David, monk
Gerasimos, monk, Nectarios, confessor; Joachim, monk
Hesychasterion of St. Euthymios at St. Neilos
Anthony, Methodios, monks of St. Neilos
Demetrios, monk, the incense-maker; Joachim, monk
Elder Sophronios, monk; Theophylactos, monk
James, monk, Gregorite
And many others.

Since the time this Proclamation was issued (1964), the monasteries, one by one, have reinstated the commemoration of the Ecumenical Patriarch's name in the services, because the monks were threatened with expulsion. Two abbots – Archimandrite Andrew of St. Paul's Monastery and Archimandrite Evdokimos of the Monastery of Xenophon – who refused to submit to force and again to commemorate the Patriarch's name, were removed forcibly and exiled. At this time (1990), only the Monastery of Esphigmenou does not commemorate the Ecumenical Patriarch's name.

A PROTEST

to Patriarch Athenagoras
on the lifting of the Anathemas of 1054

December 2/15, 1965

Your Holiness,

We have inherited a legacy from the Holy Fathers that everything in the Church should be done in a legal way, unanimously,
and conforming to ancient Traditions. If any of the bishops and even
primates of one of the autocephalous churches does something
which is not in agreement with the teaching of the whole Church,
every member of the Church may protest against it. The 15th Canon
of the First and Second Council of Constantinople of the year 861
describes as "worthy to enjoy the honour which befits them among
Orthodox Christians" those bishops and clergymen who secede
from communion even with their patriarch if he publicly preaches
heresy and openly teaches it in church. In that way we are all guar-
dians of the truth of the Church, which was always protected through
the care that nothing of general importance for the Church would
be done without the consent of all.

Therefore our attitude toward various schisms outside of the
local limits of particular autocephalous churches was never determined otherwise than by the common consensus of these churches.

If in the beginning our separation from Rome was declared in
Constantinople, then later on it became a matter of concern to the
whole Orthodox world. None of the autocephalous churches, and
specifically not the highly esteemed Church of Constantinople from
which our Russian Church has received the treasure of Orthodoxy,
may change anything in this matter without the foregoing consent
of everybody. Moreover we, the bishops ruling at present, may

not make decisions with reference to the West which would disagree with the teaching of the Holy Fathers who lived before us, specifically the Saints Photios of Constantinople and Mark of Ephesus.

In the light of these principles, although being the youngest of the primates, as the head of the free autonomous part of the Church of Russia, we regard it our duty to state our categorical protest against the action of Your Holiness with reference to your simultaneous solemn declaration with the Pope of Rome in regard to the removal of the sentence of excommunication made by Patriarch Michael Cerularius in 1054.

We heard many expressions of perplexity when Your Holiness in the face of the whole world performed something quite new and uncommon to your predecessors as well as inconsistent with the 10th Canon of the Holy Apostles at your meeting with the Pope of Rome, Paul VI, in Jerusalem. We have heard that after that, many monasteries on the Holy Mount of Athos have refused to mention your name at religious services. Let us say frankly, the confusion was great. But now Your Holiness is going even further when, only by your own decision with the bishops of your Synod, you cancel the decision of Patriarch Michael Cerularius accepted by the whole Orthodox East. In that way Your Holiness is acting contrary to the attitude accepted by the whole of our Church in regard to Roman Catholicism. It is not a question of this or that evaluation of the behaviour of Cardinal Humbert. It is not a matter of a personal controversy between the Pope and the Patriarch which could be easily remedied by their mutual Christian forgiveness; no, the essence of the problem is in the deviation from Orthodoxy which took root in the Roman Church during the centuries, beginning with the doctrine of the infallibility of the Pope which was definitively formulated at the First Vatican Council. The declaration of Your Holiness and the Pope with good reason recognises your gesture of "mutual pardon" as insufficient to end both old and more recent differences. But more than that, your gesture puts a sign of equality between error and truth. For centuries all the Orthodox Church believed with good reason that it has violated no doctrine of the Holy Ecumenical Councils; whereas the Church of Rome has introduced a number of innovations in its dogmatic teaching. The more such innovations were introduced, the deeper was to become the separation between the East and the West. The doctrinal deviations of Rome in the eleventh century did not yet contain the errors that were added later. Therefore, the cancellation of the mutual excommunication of 1054 could have been of meaning at that time, but now it is only an evidence of indifference in regard to the most important errors, namely new doctrines foreign to the ancient Church, of which some, having been exposed by St. Mark of Ephesus, were the reason why the Church rejected the Union of Florence.

We declare firmly and categorically:

No union of the Roman Church with us is possible until it renounces its new doctrines, and no communion in prayer can be restored with it without a decision of all churches, which, however, can hardly be possible before the liberation of the Church of Russia which at present has to live in catacombs. The hierarchy which is now under Patriarch Alexis cannot express the true voice of the Russian Church because it is under full control of the godless government. Primates of some other churches in countries dominated by communists also are not free.

Whereas the Vatican is not only a religious center but also a state, and whereas relations with it have also a political nature, as is evident from the visit of the Pope to the United Nations, one must reckon with the possibility of an influence in some sense of the godless authorities in the matter of the Church of Rome. History testifies to the fact that negotiations with the heterodox under pressure of political factors never brought the Church anything but confusion and schisms. Therefore we find it necessary to make a statement that our Russian Orthodox Church Outside of Russia as well as, certainly, the Russian Church which is at present in the catacombs, will not consent to any "dialogues" with other confessions and beforehand rejects any compromise with them, finding union with them possible only if they accept the Orthodox Faith as it is maintained until now in the Holy, Catholic, and Apostolic Church. While this has not happened, the excommunication proclaimed by the Patriarch Michael Cerularius is still valid, and the cancelling of it by Your Holiness is an act both illegal and void.

Certainly we are not opposed to benevolent relations with representatives of other confessions as long as the truth of Orthodoxy is not betrayed. Therefore our Church in due time accepted the invitation to send its observers to the Second Vatican Council, as well as it used to send observers to the Assemblies of the World Council of Churches, in order to have firsthand information in regard to the work of these assemblies without any participation in their deliberations.

We appreciate the kind reception of our observers, and we are studying with interest their reports showing that many changes are being introduced into the Roman Church. We will thank God if these changes will serve the cause of bringing it closer to Orthodoxy. However, if Rome has much to change in order to return to the "expression of the Faith of the Apostles," the Orthodox Church, which has maintained that Faith impeccable up to now, has nothing to change.

The Tradition of the Church and the example of the Holy Fathers teach us that the Church holds no dialogue with those who have separated themselves from Orthodoxy. Rather than that, the Church addresses to them a monologue inviting them to return to its fold through rejection of any dissenting doctrines.

A true dialogue implies an exchange of views with a possibility of persuading the participants to attain an agreement. As one can perceive from the Encyclical *"Ecclesiam Suam,"* Pope Paul VI understands the dialogue as a plan for our union with Rome with the help of some formula which would, however, leave unaltered its doctrines, and particularly its dogmatic doctrine about the position of the Pope in the Church. However, any compromise with error is foreign to the history of the Orthodox Church and to the essence of the Church. It could not bring a harmony in the confessions of the Faith, but only an illusory outward unity similar to the conciliation of dissident Protestant communities in the ecumenical movement.

May such treason against Orthodoxy not enter between us.

We sincerely ask Your Holiness to put an end to the confusion, because the way you have chosen to follow, even if it would bring you to a union with the Roman Catholics, would provoke a schism in the Orthodox world. Surely even many of your spiritual children will prefer faithfulness to Orthodoxy instead of the idea of a compromising union with the heterodox without their full harmony with us in the truth.

Asking for your prayers, I am Your Holiness' humble servant,

+ Metropolitan PHILARET
President of the Synod of Bishops
of the Russian Orthodox
Church Outside of Russia.

JUDGED BY THEIR OWN WORDS*

Quoting directly from official publications, documents and resolutions, and published sources, this article compares the teaching of those Orthodox clergymen who are involved in ecumenism with the teaching of the saints and the Ecumenical and Local Councils of the Orthodox Church.

* From the *Orthodox Christian Witness*, March 18/31, 1985, Vol. XVIII, No. 30 (833).

JUDGED BY THEIR OWN WORDS

"And the Lord said unto Him: Out of thine own
mouth will I Judge Thee "
(Cf. Luke 19:22)

As Orthodox Christians, we believe that the One, Holy, Catholic and Apostolic Church – that is, the Holy Orthodox Church – is "the Faith of the Saints" (Rev. 13: 10). Hence, every service in the Orthodox Church ends with the words: "Through the prayers of our holy Fathers, Lord Jesus Christ our God, have mercy on us. Amen." For those of us who are of the Orthodox Faith, the Holy Scriptures and Holy Tradition are actually two aspects of one, integral unit – two facets of the same thing: God's revelation to the world. And truly, it was the Holy Fathers of the Ecumenical and Local Councils who decided, by the inspiration of the Holy Spirit, which books should form the Holy Scriptures as we have them today.*

This is why the voice of the Holy Fathers means so much to us. These Saints form our unbroken and living link with Our Saviour and His Holy Apostles. They are, in truth, "the perfection of the Gospel," as the Church's hymnology calls them.

That, too, is why we are so grieved when those who call themselves Orthodox Christians brush aside or lightly dismiss the words of the Saints. We are even more grieved because, on a personal level, we are friends with many of these individuals, both clergymen and laymen, and we know

---

* For a good explanation of the Orthodox understanding of the relationship between the Holy Scriptures and Holy Tradition, see "Letters From A Convert," published by St. John of Kronstadt Press, Liberty, TN 37095.

that they are not people of evil intentions. In fact, on many occasions, many of them have shown us no little kindness, and we, in turn, have tried to be of assistance to them in whatever way we are able.

And this is as it should be.

However, the problem to which we are referring appears on another level. The problem lies in the fact that many who continue to call themselves Orthodox Christians are, in actuality, gradually being led astray from the true understanding of what the Church is. Instead of a traditional, patristic understanding of the Church, they are assimilating instead an understanding that is faulty. This particular problem seems to arise chiefly from the fact that most of these individuals are unacquainted with the lives and writings of the Fathers and Saints of the Church.

And, alas, taking advantage of this ignorance which prevails today among those who call themselves Orthodox, many "progressive" bishops and clergymen have begun to alter what we have received from the Holy Apostles and Fathers of the Church. The initial success which these "ecumenistic" clergymen have had in promoting these slight alterations – with the approval or passive acquiescence of the majority – has encouraged them to become even bolder in implementing the great plans that they have for the Church at present, and later, for all religions and all mankind.*

It would be useful for us to see how the words of these innovating clergymen and bishops contrast with the teachings of the Saints. To help our readers perceive the stark contrast that exists between the teachings of the Saints and the ecumenically-minded clergy, we would like to quote below the very words of these Orthodox (in name) clergymen, and then quote from the words of the Holy Fathers and Saints on the same subject; after this, we shall append a small commentary, if one is necessary. In this manner, we believe the contrast between the two teachings will become clear to all.

****

---

*See "The Religion of the Future," *Orthodox Christian Witness*, Feb. 4/17, 1985.

The Teaching of the Ecumenistic Clergy

In the periodical *Orthodox Observer* (30 June, 1982), which is the official publication of the Greek Archdiocese, Father George Gregory wrote the following in the feature article "Questions and Answers":

> Q. Does the Orthodox Church recognize the validity of non-Orthodox baptism?

> A. Yes. We follow the example and maintain the practice of the ancient Church on recognizing the validity of the baptism of the heretics and schismatics. However, these baptisms, to be regarded as valid, must have been celebrated in the name of the Holy Trinity and must have involved the use of water.

The Traditional Teaching of the Holy Orthodox Church

"We ordain that any bishop or presbyter who has admitted the baptism or sacrifice of heretics be deposed. For what concord hath Christ with Belial, or what part hath a believer with an infidel?"

(46th Apostolic Canon)

"Let a bishop or presbyter who shall baptize again anyone who has rightly received baptism, or who shall not baptize one who has been polluted by the ungodly [i.e. those in heresy] be deposed, as despising the Cross and death of the Lord, and not making a distinction between the true priests and the false."

(47th Apostolic Canon)

"Those baptized by heretics shall be baptized with the one true baptism in order to be admitted to the Church."

(Canon I of the Local Council of Carthage)

Comment

This is quite a contrast to what Father George Gregory tells us in the *Orthodox Observer*!

Father Gregory is apparently confused by the fact that the Church does not always baptize those who leave a heresy and come into the Church. On occasion, the Church has received non-Orthodox by chrismation, or even by the laying on of the hands, or by confession. This, however, does not mean that the Church recognizes heterodox baptisms. It simply means that, *on the condition of a non-Orthodox person asking to be received into the Church*, the Church has the power and authority to grant grace and content to that which hitherto had simply been a meaningless social rite (i.e., his heterodox "baptism"). This is emphasized by the 61st canon of the Council of Carthage in 419 A.D. which noted that "the sacraments of those *persevering in heresy* shall obtain for them the heavy penalty of eternal damnation." So, in a twisted sense, Father Gregory is right: as the 61st Canon says, heretical baptisms are "valid" and effectual, not in *saving* those who receive them, but "in obtaining for them the heavy penalty of eternal damnation."

Who needs this kind of validity?

****

The Teaching of the Ecumenistic Clergy

In the periodical *The Russian Orthodox Journal* (Nov. 1981), Archbishop Iakovos of the Greek Archdiocese said the following in an interview:

> "We do not want to leave this century divided.... Dogmatically, sacramentally, historically, we are almost Roman Catholics. We are most [sic] close to them than any other church. Now we have

to get rid of the misunderstanding caused by nine centuries."

The Teaching of the Saints of the Holy Orthodox Church

"We have cut the Latins off from us for no other reason than that they are not only schismatics, but also heretics. For this reason it is wholly improper to unite with them."

(St. Mark of Ephesus)

"Who is the antichrist?... The one is the pope and the other is he who is on our head" [i.e., the Ottoman Moslem rulers].

(St. Cosmas of Aetolia)

"The division of the churches which transpired during the time of St. Photius the Great was rather for the better, since the Church was in danger of falling away from the One Catholic and Apostolic Church (Orthodox) and becoming Roman, or rather Papal, which preaches not any longer those things of the Holy Apostles, but the dogmas of the Popes."

(St. Nectarios of Pentapolis)

Comment

In addition to the above statements of the Saints, we should add the official document referred to below. In 1583, the Pope of Rome, Gregory XIII, who changed the Julian calendar, repeatedly pressured the Patriarch of Constantinople, Jeremias, who was called the Illustrious, to follow him in the calendar innovation. The Patriarch repeatedly refused with letters, and finally in the same year, 1583, he convened a council in Constantinople at which, besides himself, were present the Patriarch of Alexandria, Sylvester, the Patriarch of Jerusalem, Sophronios, and many other bishops. This council issued a *Sigillion* which was sent to all the regional Orthodox churches and which enumerates the principal heresies of the Papacy and anathematizes (i.e., proclaims as being out of the Church) all those who profess them. (The entire text of the *Sigillion* is found on pages 92-93.)

This *Sigillion* is found in manuscript Codex 772, in the Sacred Monastery of St. Panteleimon, on the Holy Mountain, and manuscript Codex No. 285 of the cell "The Akathist Hymn" of the Sacred Skete of Kafsokalyvia, on the Holy Mountain. It was first published in 1881, in the periodical *The Roumanian Orthodox Church* in Bucharest (12th issue), by the Russian Archimandrite Porphyrius Uspensky, who copied it from a manuscript codex of the great library of Mount Sinai.

Is a clearer or more eloquent condemnation of the Papacy needed than this one? Certainly not. How, then, does Archbishop Iakovos reconcile what he believes with what the Saints and Local Councils teach? Evidently, he simply ignores or dismisses the latter.

****

The Teaching of the Ecumenistic Clergy

In his "Christmas Message," printed in the periodical *Episkepsis* (25 Dec. 1978), Demetrius, the present Ecumenical Patriarch in Constantinople, refers to Origen as a "Father of the Church," and quotes him as though he were of equal authority with St. Gregory of Nyssa and St. Gregory the Theologian.

(Origen taught, among other things, that souls pre-exist bodies, that after the death of one body, souls are reincarnated in another, that the demons will become angels, and the fires of gehenna – contrary to what our Lord Jesus Christ taught – are not eternal.)

The Traditional Teaching of the Holy Orthodox Church

"Our Fathers denounced and anathematized Origen for

perverting the truth."

(St. Cyril of Alexandria)

The doctrine of Origen is a "doctrine of wickedness which arouses in souls an unclean stench."

(The Rule of St. Pachomius the Great)

"Let all of us, and especially the fallen, beware lest we sicken in heart from the disease of the atheist Origen."

(St. John of the Divine Ladder)

And finally, the Fifth Ecumenical Council condemned both Origen and his teachings on *fifteen different counts.*

Comment

We believe no further comment is necessary here.

****

The Teaching of the Ecumenistic Clergy

In August, 1971, Patriarch Athenagoras of Constantinople met with a group of thirty Greek priests from America and five Greek priests from Germany who were visiting the Ecumenical Patriarchate. His words to the priests were published in the periodical *Orthodoxos Typos* (13 July, 1979). Here is an excerpt of the Patriarch's speech:

> "And what is taking place today? A great spirit of love is spreading abroad over the Christians of the East and West. Already we love one another . . . already in America you give communion to many from the holy chalice, and you do well! And I also here, when Catholics and Protestants come and ask to receive

communion, I offer them the holy cup! And in Rome the same thing is happening, and in England, and in France. Already it is coming by itself."

And also:

On December 16, 1969, the Holy Synod of the Moscow Patriarchate made the official decision to permit Roman Catholics in the Soviet Union to receive communion from Orthodox priests. This practice continues to this day without Roman Catholics first being required to renounce the heresies of the Papacy and then to be joined to the Church by chrismation or baptism.[*]

And also:

The Thyateira Confession, by Archbishop Athenagoras Kokkinakis of Thyateira and Great Britain, was printed "With the Blessing and Authorization of the Ecumenical Patriarchate of Constantinople" in 1975. In his letter of commendation of *The Thyateira Confession* (Jan. 10, 1975), Ecumenical Patriarch Demetrius wrote the following:

"This Study [i.e., *The Thyateira Confession*] has been examined by the Synodical Committee of the Patriarchate and has been found appropriate for the care of the spiritual needs of the rational flock which is entrusted to the care of Your Eminence. In addition it has been considered as a fit aid even for our own Catechists and for the benefit of the non-Orthodox who desire to receive general information concerning our Orthodox Church.

"Gladly therefore according to the Decision of the Synod We extend our Blessing for the Publication of this excellent work, the product of pastoral zeal and the spiritual endurance of Your

---

[*]In an interview reported in the *Ecumenical Press Service* (April 11-25, 1990), Archbishop Kirill of Smolensk (Soviet Patriarchate) affirmed: "I am deeply convinced that the Ukrainian Catholics enjoy sacramental communion with the Orthodox in Western Ukraine." (Editor's Note)

Eminence and congratulate you wholeheartedly on its production."

On page 69 of this *Thyateira Confession*, which bears the official approval of the Church of Constantinople, we read:

"When they are not near a Roman Catholic Church, Roman Catholics are permitted to receive the Holy Communion in Orthodox Churches; and the same is also extended to Orthodox when they are not near an Orthodox Church."

"It is now permissible for Orthodox and Roman Catholics to pray together, and for the Orthodox Liturgy to be offered in a Roman Catholic Church. Parallel permission is now granted by some Orthodox Churches for the celebration of the Catholic Mass in Orthodox churches."*

---

* In December of 1983, Patriarch Demetrius issued an encyclical stating that it was not permitted to give communion to non-Orthodox "on the basis of the Encyclical of March 14, 1967." However, in 1971, Patriarch Athenagoras, who issued the aforementioned Encyclical of 1967, admitted with pride that he gave communion to both Roman Catholics and Protestants. This means either one of two things: 1) On the basis of his own Encyclical, Patriarch Athenagoras should have been suspended or defrocked – as the canons specify, or, 2) Despite the fact that he issued it, Patriarch Athenagoras did not attach any importance to this particular Encyclical.

Since Patriarch Athenagoras was not defrocked, or even reprimanded, we are forced to conclude that the second instance must be true. Our conclusion in this matter is fortified by the fact that the Ecumenical Patriarchate has not officially condemned the book *The Thyateira Confession*, which it officially recommended in 1975, and which openly permits "inter-communion" between Roman Catholics and Orthodox. If it is a violation of the Orthodox Faith to give communion to non-Orthodox, then what can we say regarding all those years (1975-1983) when the Ecumenical Patriarchate was supporting "Inter-communion" officially? On an unofficial basis, Patriarch Athenagoras – by his own admission – was practicing Inter-communion at least as early as 1971, and the Moscow Patriarchate has been doing so officially since 1969.

If Patriarch Demetrius' Encyclical of 1983 is to be taken as a serious and official statement (and one can only hope that it is taken seriously – at least, more seriously than the Encyclical of 1967), then we must ask: Have the bishops who were responsible for the former policy been suspended or defrocked, as the canons specify? Have they, at least, made a public apology? If nothing else, were they reprimanded and given an *epitimion*?

None of these has occurred.

Surely, if the Ecumenical Patriarchate wishes to be recognized as a "canonical Orthodox church," then It has to make some effort to abide by the canons and the doctrines of the Orthodox Church.

"Let a bishop, presbyter, or deacon who has only prayed with
heretics be excommunicated; but if he has permitted them to
perform any clerical office, let him be deposed."

(45th Apostolic Canon)

"Whosoever has communion with one who is excommunicated
is to be excommunicated, as one who brings confusion into the
order of the Church."

(10th Apostolic Canon)

The same canon is reiterated by the councils of Antioch (2nd Canon),
of Carthage (9th Canon), by St. Mark of Ephesus (PG 160, 97C), and St.
Symeon Metaphrastes ("Epistle of Canons," PG 114, 260).

"All the teachers of the Church, all the Synods, and all the Sacred
Scriptures admonish the faithful to flee from those that teach
heresy, and they forbid them to have communion with them."

(St. Mark of Ephesus)

"With a great voice, St. John Chrysostom addressed as enemies
of God not only the heretics, but also those who were in communion with them."

(St. Theodore the Studite)

Of course, when the Church Fathers speak of "communion" with
the heterodox, they are not referring only to the Eucharist, but also to
communion or fellowship in prayer.

Also, at this point, it would be useful for us to remember that all
Orthodox Christians use the Divine Liturgy of St. John Chrysostom. It
is evident, however, from the documents that we have quoted that some
present-day "Orthodox" patriarchs, bishops and priests do not agree with

St. John Chrysostom in matters of the Faith.

"Is the shepherd a heretic? Then he is a wolf! Flee from him; do not be deceived by him even if he appears gentle and tame. Avoid communion with him even as you would flee from a poisonous snake."

(St. Photius the Great, Patriarch of Constantinople)

And since we are speaking here primarily concerning Roman Catholicism, the words of St. Mark of Ephesus, which we quoted previously, could be repeated:

"We have cut the Latins off from us for no other reason than that they are not only schismatics, but also heretics. For this reason it is wholly improper to unite with them."

Comment

Since the time these words were spoken, has the Roman Catholic Church renounced any of its errors? Not at all. To the contrary, it has added even more, for example, the doctrine of papal infallibility. So what has changed? Certainly, the teachings of the Orthodox Church have not changed. This leads us to but one inescapable conclusion: The contemporary bishops and priests of the Greek Archdiocese, the Patriarchate of Constantinople, and the Moscow Patriarchate, whom we have quoted *verbatim* above, no longer teach what the Orthodox Catholic Church teaches.

****

This is not the first time that a Patriarch of Constantinople or bishops attached to the Ecumenical Throne have fallen into a heretical teaching. One prominent example was Nestorius, who was condemned by the Third Ecumenical Council in 431. Also, the Sixth Ecumenical Council in 681 condemned four Patriarchs of Constantinople, as well as one Pope of Rome, one Patriarch of Alexandria, and a Patriarch of Antioch for heresy.

Patriarch Athenagoras, and the present-day Patriarch of Constantinople, Demetrius, as well as the hierarchs attached to his See, and also
the Moscow Patriarchate, have obviously placed themselves above the
Apostles and Saints. If we understand their words correctly, they apparently believe that "the great spirit of love is spreading abroad" in our
own days (when materialism, secularism, atheism and immorality have
reached unprecedented heights!) and that the Apostles and Saints lacked
this "great spirit of love" when they warned us against praying and having
communion with the heterodox.

However, from our God and Saviour, and from His Holy Apostles,
Prophets, Martyrs, Hierarchs, Righteous Fathers, and Confessors, we
have learned that, above all else, we are to treasure and preserve intact our
Orthodox Faith, which was revealed from on high. "Stand fast and hold
the traditions which ye have been taught, whether by mouth or by epistle,"
cries the Holy Apostle Paul to the Thessalonians. To the Galatians he
wrote, "Though we or an angel from Heaven preach any other Gospel unto
you than that which we have preached unto you, let him be anathema." And
St. John the Evangelist, the Beloved Disciple of our Lord, and Apostle of
Love *par excellence*, exhorts us not even to greet a man who has distorted
the Holy Faith and who persists in trying to preach his errors and personal
opinions to us.

How can we, therefore, who profess to be Orthodox Christians, ignore
these admonitions which are found in the Holy Scriptures themselves? If
these words were spoken by men who were filled with the Holy Spirit and
whose souls overflowed with love for both God and man, how can we dare
to ignore them and foolishly follow after bishops and clergymen who do
not hesitate to disdain and overthrow even the teachings of our Saviour
and His Apostles? Shall we not thus forfeit our eternal salvation?

We shall be the first to rejoice when these aforementioned clergymen retract their ecumenistic teachings and begin again to teach with
the words of the Apostles and Fathers. We shall be the first to embrace
them, to ask for their blessing, and to join in prayer and communion with
them. But so long as they insist on following their own path apart from
the Fathers, Apostles and Saints, and in praying and in having "inter-
communion" with the heterodox* there is no way that we will ever consent

* In all the writings and decrees of the holy Fathers and holy Councils, the term
"intercommunion" Is nowhere to be found. One is either in communion with

to pray or to have communion with them. As we have demonstrated from their own words, the responsibility for this separation rests on them and them alone.

In the meantime, as Orthodox Christians, we must remain faithful to "sound doctrine" as the Holy Apostle admonishes us, no matter what else may come to pass. With love and with persistence, we shall continue to follow St. Paul's advice to Timothy:

> "Preach the word; be ready in season, out of season; reprove, rebuke, exhort with all long-suffering and teaching. For the time will come when they will not endure sound doctrine; but, having itching ears, they shall heap up unto themselves teachers according to their own desires; and they shall turn away their ears from the truth, and shall be turned aside unto fables."
>
> (11 Timothy 4:2-4)

Through the prayers of our holy Fathers, Lord Jesus Christ our God, have mercy on us. Amen.

the One, Holy, Catholic and Apostolic Church, or one is out of communion with the Church (i.e., excommunicated). How can there be such a thing as "inter-communion between the Churches" when there is only One Church in the first place? Is Christ divided? Is the Body of Christ – that is, the Church-divided? If the Church is divided, this means that the Body of Christ is divided; this means that the gates of Hell have prevailed against the Church, and therefore Our Saviour has proved to be a false prophet.

Obviously, whoever first conceived the so-called "Branch Theory" was not a Christian.

A QUESTION OF INTEGRITY

The representative of the Ecumenical Patriarch addressed St. Maximus: "Will you enter into communion with our Church, or not?"

"No, I will not enter into communion," replied the Saint.

"Why?" inquired the representative.

"Because she has rejected the rulings of the Orthodox councils," replied the Saint.

"But if our Church has renounced the councils," objected the representative, "then how is it that they are inscribed in the diptychs?"

"What profit is there in naming them and recalling them, if the dogmas of these councils are rejected?" was the Saint's reply.

"Can you demonstrate clearly," asked the representative, "that the present Church at Constantinople has rejected the dogmas of the former councils?"

"If you refrain from anger, and command me to do so, I can demonstrate it easily," replied the Saint.[1]

-BASIC TEACHINGS-

Some months ago, an interesting feature article, the "Religious Question Box" appeared in the July 18, 1985 issue of the *Hellenic Chronicle*, a Greek-American newspaper published in Boston, Massachusetts. This feature article is written by the Rev. Dr. Stanley S. Harakas, a faculty member of Holy Cross Seminary in Brookline, Massachusetts and former dean of the school.

[1] *The Life of Our Holy Father Maximus the Confessor,* translated by Fr. Christopher Birchall, Boston, Mass., 1982, pp. 43-4.

In many ways, this particular article is highly commendable. In other ways, it is remarkable for what it omits.

We would like to quote some of the more pertinent parts of this article:

> Q. A non-Orthodox Christian may not receive Holy Communion in the Orthodox Church. Why? G.D., Biloxi, Miss.
>
> A. I could answer your question by quoting a number of Church canons. That would formally support the statement which you made. I would rather try to make the position of the Church clear and understandable in terms of the inner logic and rationale of the Church's self-understanding.
>
> The Nature of the Church:
>
> We begin by noting the nature of the Church. The Church is the body of Christ. The Orthodox Church has always seen itself as being the "one, holy, catholic and apostolic" Church of Christ in all of its fullness. Thus, for an individual Christian to be in communion with the "one, holy, catholic and apostolic" Church is an either-or proposition: either you are a member or you are not.
>
> The Chief Signs of Membership in the Church:
>
> Acceptance of the teachings of the Church by believers is an important sign of membership. This has never meant that believers had to be theologians, or highly informed regarding the subtleties of the faith. The basic teachings about God, Christ, the Sacraments, the Church and the Last Things are what is meant here. All these are summarized in the Creed. If a believer can repeat the Creed in faith, he or she shares in this "sign of membership."

It is at this point exactly that Fr. Stanley's explanation gets sidetracked. When he writes: "Acceptance of the teachings of the Church by believers is an important sign of membership," Fr. Stanley is absolutely correct. But he is absolutely wrong when he goes on to qualify his statement as follows: "The basic teachings about God, Christ, the Sacraments, the Church and the Last Things are what is meant here."

Contrary to what Fr. Stanley writes, the Orthodox Church does not make any such distinctions as "basic" or "non-basic" when speaking about her teachings.

In fact, this is exactly the point that was made by the Orthodox delegates at the WCC General Assembly in Evanston, Illinois, in 1954. Here is what the Orthodox delegates said in their *Declaration*:

The whole of the Christian Faith should be regarded as one, indivisible unity. It is not enough to accept just certain, particular doctrines as basic as they may be in themselves, e.g., that Christ is God and Savior. It is necessary that all doctrines as formulated by the Ecumenical Councils, as well as the totality of the teachings of the Early, Undivided Church should be accepted.

In addition, the Orthodox statement "The Nature of the Unity We Seek" issued at the WCC Faith & Order Study Conference in Oberlin, Ohio in 1957 went on to say:

Any agreement on faith must rest on the authority of the statements of the seven Ecumenical Councils which represent the mind of the one undivided Church of antiquity and the subsequent tradition as safeguarded in the life of the Orthodox Church.

As Fr. Stanley writes, our membership in the Church has nothing to do with whether or not we are "theologians" or "highly informed concerning the subtleties of the faith." But, contrary to what Fr. Stanley says, our membership in the Body of Christ certainly does depend on whether or not we accept and uphold *all* of the Church's teachings with faith and to the best of our ability.

For example, how many of us understand or can explain the manner in which the bread and wine in the Holy Eucharist are changed into the very Body and Blood of our Saviour? No one, of course. Nonetheless, this mystery is a "basic" tenet of the Christian Faith, and we are duty-bound to accept it and defend it — even though no mention whatsoever is made of it in the Creed.

There are many such "basic" tenets of our Orthodox Faith which are not mentioned in the Creed, e.g. "Theotokos," the sign of the cross, the holy icons. Can one be even "basically" Orthodox without accepting these? And what of the *Synodicon* of Orthodoxy Sunday which condemns the heresies of the Arians, Nestorians, Monophysites, and even many heretical teachings which are now taught by Roman Catholics and Protestants? The *Synodicon* also is a basic statement of the Orthodox Faith.

When we define the "chief signs of membership in the Church" as the acceptance of "basic" teachings, all of which, according to Fr. Stanley, "are summarized in the Creed," then we shall find ourselves sharing "a common cup" with a very wide spectrum of "fellow-believers."

For example, the Uniates recite the Nicene Creed — presumably "with faith". Is this a sign that they are members of the Orthodox Church and may receive communion with us? On occasion, the Pope of Rome also has been known to recite the original Nicene Creed without the "Filioque" clause. Does this mean that we may give him communion on those particular occasions? Sometimes the Anglicans and even some conservative Protestant bodies do the same as an "ecumenical gesture" towards their "Orthodox brethren." Under those circumstances, may the Orthodox Christian receive the "consecrated bread and wine" from the hands of an Anglican priest or priestess?

Then again, could this "basic" Faith also be the reason why Bishop Kallistos Ware of England (with whom Fr. Stanley is in communion) has given communion to Monophysites, who have no difficulty in reciting the Nicene Creed "in faith"? At the same time, however, the Monophysites obdurately refuse to obey the decrees of the last four Ecumenical Councils. But, according to the criterion provided by Fr. Stanley in his article, the matters those Ecumenical Councils dealt with are not included in what is "basic" to the Orthodox Faith. [2]

Finally, we note that even the Unitarians recite the Nicene Creed once a year "for historical reasons."

[2] One is tempted to ask: if Fr. Stanley does believe that the decisions of

How quickly our church membership expands when we get down to the "basics"!

Indeed, were we to make only one or two very slight alterations in the Creed, we could begin giving communion to Moslems also!

A Freemason's dream come true!

Needless to say, however, Fr. Stanley is completely in error in his definition of the "signs of church membership." In contrast, the Orthodox statements at Evanston and Oberlin — which we quoted above — provide us with the true criterion of membership in the Body of Christ:

> It is necessary that *all* doctrines as formulated by the Ecumenical Councils...should be accepted.

And:

> Any agreement on faith must rest on the authority of the enactments of the *Seven Ecumenical Councils*...and the subsequent tradition as safeguarded in the life of the Orthodox Church.

– A CANONICAL ORTHODOX BISHOP –

This brings us to the next section of Fr. Stanley's article. Fr. Stanley writes:

> In addition to orthodoxy of belief, is communion with a canonical Bishop, that is, membership in a local church body which is in communion with all of the other canonical Orthodox churches in the world. Being under the canonical and spiritual care of a Bishop who is in communion with all the other canonical Orthodox churches is a "sign of membership" which is extremely important. It not only unites us with all other Orthodox throughout the world today, but it also unites us with the historical body of the Church through the centuries. Today's Orthodox are one

the Seven Ecumenical Councils are binding — and we prefer to believe that he does — then why is he in communion with a bishop who gives communion to individuals who disdain and even anathematize the last four Ecumenical Councils?

with the Church of Christ, the Apostles, the Fathers of every age and place and with the Church Triumphant of the saints.

What Fr. Stanley has written here is absolutely correct, and no Orthodox Christian could object to what he has said. When he writes that a "sign of membership in the Church" is "communion with a canonical bishop, that is, membership in a local church body which is in communion with all the other canonical Orthodox churches in the world," the two key words here, obviously, are "canonical" and "Orthodox". Fr. Stanley emphasizes that communion with a "canonical Orthodox" bishop is "extremely important."

Now an "extremely important" question arises: Is a bishop canonical or Orthodox when — contrary to every holy canon and in defiance of all Orthodox Christian doctrine — he participates in joint-prayer services with the non-Orthodox under ecumenical auspices, or gives communion to non-Orthodox?

Of course not.

How can one be canonical while, at the same time, trampling the holy canons underfoot? And how can a bishop be Orthodox while, contrary to Orthodox doctrine, he gives communion to those who do not believe what the Orthodox Church believes?

Fr. Stanley himself refers to the importance of the holy canons in the very beginning of his article, when he writes: "I could answer your question by quoting a number of Church canons. That would formally support the statement which you made [regarding the fact that a non-Orthodox may not receive Holy Communion in the Orthodox Church]."

Such being the case, Fr. Stanley has just placed himself in the unenviable position of having condemned his own bishops for being both uncanonical and un-Orthodox!

The holy canons strictly forbid joint-prayer services with non-Orthodox. Yet, in total defiance of the canons, every bishop of the Ecumenical Patriarchate — including Patriarch Demetrios and Archbishop Iakovos — and all the other "canonical Orthodox" jurisdictions which are members of the World Council of Churches repeatedly participate in these joint-prayer services.

So much for the canonicity of Fr. Stanley's "canonical" hierarchy...[3]

As for the question of Orthodoxy, we are sure that Fr. Stanley would agree that one cannot be Orthodox if he is in communion with the non-Orthodox. For example, St. Mark of Ephesus tells us: "All the teachers of the Church, all the Councils, and all the Sacred Scriptures admonish the faithful to flee from those that teach heresy, and they forbid them to have communion with them." And St. Theodore the Studite adds, "St. John Chrysostom addressed as enemies of God not only the heretics, but also those who are in communion with them."

Now the question arises: are the Roman Catholics Orthodox? Of course not. They are members of a denomination encumbered with all the innovations and heresies that are part and parcel of the Papacy. Are then the Protestants Orthodox? No, there is no way that they are Orthodox. What of the Monophysites? Are they Orthodox? Insofar as they stubbornly refuse to accept "the enactments of the seven Ecumenical Councils,... and the subsequent tradition as safeguarded in the life of the Orthodox Church," no, they too cannot be considered Orthodox, even though they are the closest to us in their beliefs and ethos.

If this is the case, how then can Fr. Stanley justify the fact that he is in submission to bishops who give communion to Roman Catholics, Protestants and Monophysites? The late Patriarch Athenagoras boasted that he gave communion to both Roman Catholics and Protestants.[4] In

---

[3] On one occasion, a Greek Archdiocese priest was speaking with a priest of our jurisdiction. The Greek priest remonstrated with our priest: "You people are always accusing us of breaking the canons. Well, the canons also forbid a priest to dispense communion with a spoon. So you're breaking the canons too." To which our priest replied, "I'll tell you what. Lets make an agreement. I'll agree to stop giving communion with a spoon, if you agree to stop praying with heretics!" Unfortuntely, the Greek priest did not agree to this "contract." Needless to say, however, these two canons are quite dissimilar in their import and purpose. The first has to do with the church's inner discipline, whereas the other — regarding prayers with non-Orthodox — has to do with the Church's doctrinal integrity. This is precisely what the Orthodox statement, " The Nature of the Unity We Seek," pointed out: "In order to safeguard the unity of the faith and the integrity of the liturgical and spiritual life of the Orthodox Church, abstinence from inter-denominational activities is encouraged on a local level."

England, Archbishop Methodios, who is under the Ecumenical Patriarchate, has done the same. Bishop Kallistos Ware, by his own admission, has given communion to the Monophysites. Within the Soviet Union, the Moscow Patriarchate gives communion to Roman Catholics "when no church of their own is nearby." In his book, *The Thyateira Confession*, Archbishop Athenagoras Kokkinakis, with the *official* approval of Patriarch Demetrios and his Synod, writes that it is permitted for Roman Catholics to receive communion from the Orthodox, and vice versa.

So much for the Orthodoxy of Fr. Stanley's "Orthodox" hierarchy... [5]

Fr. Stanley is correct. It is "extremely important" that we be in communion with a "canonical Orthodox bishop," for this "unites us with the historical body of the Church through the centuries." And he continues, "Today's Orthodox are one with the Church of Christ, the Apostles, the Fathers of every age and place."

The only problem for Fr. Stanley, and with those who are in communion with his hierarchy, is that his jurisdiction — thanks to its ecumenistic ecclesiology and to declarations such as *The Thyateira Confession* — is no longer representative of "today's Orthodox," for the "Fathers of every age and place" did not pray with and give communion to the non-Orthodox as Fr. Stanley's hierarchs do — by their own admission.

It is not enough to be in communion with a "historical see," because even "historical sees" have had their un-Orthodox periods at some point in the past. Rome, too, was a "historical see" — but this is of no avail to her today. Constantinople also has had her staunchly heretical days. For three and a half years, Nestorios ruled as Patriarch of Constantinople until he was condemned for heresy and deposed by the Third Ecumenical Council in 431. In the seventh century, during the Monothelite controversy, the Ecumenical Patriarchate was in the camp of the non-Orthodox for almost eighty years. Finally, in 681, the Sixth Ecumenical Council was convened and condemned four Patriarchs of Constantinople, one Patriarch of Alexandria, two Patriarchs of Antioch, a multitude of other Metropolitans, Archbishop, Bishops, clergymen, and also one Pope of

[4] See "Judged By Their Own Words", p.111.
[5] Please see footnote on page 120.

Rome for heresy. Again, in the eighth century, during the Iconoclast controversy, for the better part of the century, Constantinople was again in heresy and not an Orthodox church.

When the Monothelite heresy was raging, St. Maximus the Confessor was Orthodoxy's foremost champion. Here is what the Saint said then about the Ecumenical Patriarchate:

> When I see the Church of Constantinople as she was formerly, then I will enter into communion with her without any exhortation on the part of men. But when there are heretical temptations in her, and while heretics are her bishops, no word or deed will convince me ever to enter into communion with her. [6]

In a parallel case today, Orthodox Christians are often reproached for isolating themselves from "official" Patriarchates, from "World Orthodoxy" (such as the Ecumenical Patriarchate to which Fr. Stanley belongs), as if not being in communion with them were itself a sign that these Orthodox Christians are not canonical or Orthodox.

There is only one problem with this argument: *nowhere* do the holy canons state that one has to be in communion with any of the aforementioned Patriarchates in order for one to be Orthodox! Fr. Stanley could not quote any canons to support this "extremely important" point of his article simply because there are no such canons!

But let us permit St. Maximus the Confessor to provide us with truly "canonical Orthodox" guidelines for responding to these reproaches which our Orthodox Christians sometimes hear.

The Saint was asked by his inquisitors (who belonged to the Ecumenical Patriarchate):

> To which church do you belong? To that of Byzantium, Rome, Antioch, Alexandria, or Jerusalem? For all of these churches, together with the provinces in subjection to them, are in unity. Therefore, if you also belong to the Catholic Church, enter into communion with us at once.... Yesterday, indeed, two delegates

---

[6] *The Life of Our Holy Father Maximus the Confessor,* op. cit., p. 20.

arrived from Rome, and tomorrow, the Lord's day, they will communicate the Holy Mysteries with the Ecumenical Patriarch.[7]

To this, St. Maximus replied as follows to the representatives of the Ecumenical Patriarchate (and to all those who present themselves as the spokesmen of "official" Orthodoxy):

> *Even if the whole universe* holds communion with the Patriarch, I will not communicate with him. For I know from the writings of the holy Apostle Paul: the Holy Spirit declares that even the angels would be anathema if they should begin to preach another Gospel, introducing some new teaching.

The "new teaching" of St. Maximus' day was Monothelitism. The "new teaching" of our own times is Ecumenism. Today's Ecumenism — and its ecclesiological and theological prop, the Branch Theory — is what permits the bishops and clergy of "World Orthodoxy" to have joint-prayer services with and give communion to non-Orthodox — which is, of course, not Orthodox.

Unfortunately for the proponents of Ecumenism, however, the heresies of the Roman Catholics, Protestants, and Monophysites have been condemned repeatedly in the decisions of the seven Ecumenical Councils, in the *Synodicon* of Orthodoxy Sunday, and in many other subsequent local Orthodox councils. Hence, no matter how much the ecumenically-minded Orthodox try to re-interpret Orthodox ecclesiology, the fact remains that they are in communion and pray with clergymen who are adherents of condemned heresies.

As Fr. Stanley says at the end of his article:

Now you see why a non-Orthodox may not receive Holy Communion in the Orthodox Church. It is a question of integrity. The integrity of faith, church order, lifestyle and sacramental life.

This is precisely what Orthodox Christians have been saying for some twenty years to those Orthodox who are of an ecumenical turn of mind: It is a question of integrity. Hence, when ecumenistic "Orthodox" bishops

---

[7] *The Life of Our Holy Father Maximus the Confessor,* op. cit., pp. 14,38.

and clergy have joint-prayer services with the heterodox and give them communion, they are being neither "canonical" nor "Orthodox." Under such circumstances, surely, they lose their "integrity of faith, church order, lifestyle and sacramental life."

In this, Fr. Stanley is absolutely correct.

THE FORM OF HOLY BAPTISM

by His Grace Bishop Ephraim of Boston

In the Name of the Father, and of the Son, and of the Holy Spirit. Amen.

"Unless a man be born of water and the Spirit, he cannot enter into the Kingdom of God" (John 3:5). Why not? Because, as Saint John Chrysostom answers, "he wears the garment of death, of cursing, of perdition, he has not yet received his Lord's insignia, he is a stranger and an alien, he does not have the royal watchword."[1]

Baptism has become a particularly vital issue of late, even in ecumenical circles. Wherever one stands on other issues regarding the Christian Faith, be he Protestant, Roman Catholic, or Orthodox Christian, all agree that Baptism is necessary for membership in the Church. This is quite natural, for our Saviour Himself declares unequivocally: "Unless a man be born of water and the Spirit, he cannot enter into the Kingdom of God" (John 3:5).

The Church Fathers, in fact, felt so strongly about the absolute necessity of Baptism that the Sixth Ecumenical Council, in its Eighty-fourth Canon, specified that if anyone "does not know or can prove by documents that he has been baptized, he must without any hesitation be baptized"—even at the risk of being baptized a second time. That's how important this Mystery is.

However, after this initial agreement concerning the need for Bap-

---

[1] St. John Chrysostom, *On the Gospel of Saint John*, Homily Twenty-five.

tism, there is a general breakdown of concord on virtually every other point in regard to Holy Baptism: Is water absolutely necessary? Is water that which effects our regeneration, or is it only a symbol of that regeneration? Should infants be baptized? Does our faith have anything to do with Baptism? If so, to what degree? Is it necessary to have the Orthodox Faith to be baptized? Is there Baptism outside the Church? If so, then where are the borders of the Church? Does the Church accept the validity of "baptism" performed by the heterodox, and if so, under what conditions? If not, why not? Is the form as well as the content of the Holy Mystery of Baptism important? In whose name are we baptized?

These questions are not new. The Church has had to deal with these very questions right from the very beginning. For those of us who are Orthodox Christians, it is a comfort to know that all of these problems have been dealt with in antiquity. All that is left for us to do is to take the time and make the effort to search out what the early Church writers had to say on these issues. Basically, there is no need for us to hammer out our own personal solutions to these vexing matters, since God-inspired men, following in the footsteps of the Apostles and their disciples, have already resolved these questions. The only thing that is required of us is to uphold their Apostolic teachings.

Of course, it is not possible, in the space here allotted, to deal with all of the questions listed above. The task that is assigned to us here is to examine more specifically the actual form of Christian Baptism and its theological implications.

Several elements are necessary if the Mystery of Holy Baptism is to be imparted in its correct form. These elements are:

(1) Immersion in water.
(2) The invocation of the Holy Trinity.
(3) The correct Faith.
(4) The Holy Spirit.

Since Fr. Michael Azkoul will speak on the role of the Holy Spirit in Baptism and Chrismation, we need not consider this particular topic here. But in considering the first three points we will see from many apostolic and patristic sources how much importance was attached to the proper and traditional form of Baptism. This concern for the correct form did not arise from petty hair-splitting. It came, rather, from the belief that the form represents a statement of faith, a conviction, a vital belief of the Church. It is a visible application and demonstration of the Church's doctrine.

In contrast to this necessary concern for the correct form, there is, even among those who are nominally Orthodox (not to mention the heterodox), often a grievous laxity in properly performing the Mystery of Baptism. This laxity is in fact so pronounced as sometimes to leave one wondering whether a "baptism" actually took place. In some instances, for example, vessels that bear the name "baptismal font" are hardly deep enough to baptize the baby's ankles, let alone the baby. This is really inexcusable, especially since—as I noted above and as we shall see further below—the Church has always been so concerned about this matter, in view of the fact that the form itself is the visible application of Christian teaching.

Immersion in Water

The importance of water in Baptism is evident in the Holy Scriptures themselves. For example, in the Gospel of Saint John we read:

> After these things, Jesus and His disciples came into the land of Judæa; and there He tarried with them, and baptized. And John also was baptizing in Ænon near to Salim, because there was much water there.
>
> John 3:23

Saint Paul also gives another important insight into the correct form of Holy Baptism. He writes:

> Know ye not that as many of us as were baptized into Jesus Christ were baptized into His death? Therefore, we are buried with Him by baptism into death, so that like as Christ was raised up from the dead by the glory of the Father, even so we also should walk in newness of life. For if we have been planted together in the likeness of His death, we shall be also in the likeness of His resurrection.
>
> Romans 6:3–5

In his first Epistle, moreover, Saint Peter makes allusion to the importance of water—indeed, a great deal of water—when, immediately after he speaks of the time of Noah and the flood, and how those who were with Noah were saved by water, Saint Peter goes on to say:

> There is also an antitype which now saveth us, namely Baptism.
>
> I Peter 3:21

Again, in the Acts of the Apostles, we see a description of the Baptism of the eunuch of Candace, the queen of Ethiopia. The Acts describe how Philip and the eunuch were travelling down the road in a chariot while Saint Philip spoke to him of the Messiah. Then it says:

> As they went down the road, they came to a certain body of water. And the eunuch said, "Behold, water! What hinders me from being baptized?" And Philip said, "If you believe with all your heart, you may." And he answered and said, "I believe that Jesus Christ is the Son of God." And he commanded the chariot to stand still. And both Philip and the eunuch went down into the water, and he baptized him. And when they had come up out of the water, the Spirit of the Lord caught Philip away, so that the eunuch saw him no more; and he went on his way rejoicing.
>
> Acts 8:36–39

As we see in these passages, the element of water—lots of water—is very important.

In the generation that followed the holy Apostles we likewise have an abundance of testimonies regarding the Church's Baptism. In fact, the texts are far too numerous to quote more than a few especially significant ones here. Among these is a passage in *The Shepherd of Hermas*, written around the year 100, that is, only some ten years after the repose of Saint John the Evangelist.

This work consists of three large sections: the first is divided into five chapters called Visions; the second into twelve chapters called Mandates; and the third into ten chapters called Parables. In the Ninth Parable, we read the following:

They had need [said the Shepherd] to come up through the water, so that they might be made alive; for they could not otherwise enter into the Kingdom of God, except by putting away the mortality of their former life. These also, then, who have fallen asleep, received the seal of the Son of God, and entered into the Kingdom of God. For, he said, before a man bears the Name of the Son of God, he is dead. But when he receives the seal, he puts mortality aside and again receives life. The seal, therefore, is the water. They go down into the water dead, and come out of it alive.[2]

This passage, like the one which we just saw in Saint Paul's Epistle to the Romans, gives another insight into the theological aspect of the water of baptism as an image of death. We shall return to this theme shortly.

Another second century document that speaks of the form of Baptism is the *Didache*, or Teaching of the Twelve Apostles. (This document makes reference to the work which was just quoted, that is, *The Shepherd of Hermas*.) Most scholars agree that it was written no later than 160 A.D., and, most likely, much earlier. As its name suggests, the *Didache* contains many teachings of the Apostles which were passed down and finally codified in this text.

Concerning Baptism, the *Didache* has this to say:

In regard to Baptism—baptize thus: After the foregoing instructions, baptize in the Name of the Father, and of the Son, and of the Holy Spirit, in living water. If you have no living water, then baptize in other water; and if you are not able in cold, then in warm. If you have neither, pour three times on the head, in the Name of the Father, and of the Son, and of the Holy Spirit. Before the Baptism, let the one baptizing and the one to be baptized fast, as also any others who are able. Command the one who is to be baptized to fast beforehand for one or two days.[3]

Here we see how an alternate form of Baptism is provided for, with, however, the specific qualification that such an alternate may be used only when the prescribed and traditional form cannot be used for some good reason. The Church maintains this use of an alternate form of Baptism, in,

[2] *The Shepherd of Hermas*, Parable Nine, 16, 2.
[3] *Didache*, 7, 1.

for example, the case of clinical Baptisms, or in other cases where no water at all is available and one is in danger of dying without Baptism. Nonetheless, in such cases, the Church also specifies that, if the person lives, such "special" or emergency Baptisms must be perfected and "regularized" at the first opportunity—that is, set aright according to the prescribed and canonical order.

But here we have been talking for so long about Baptism, and we have not yet examined the exact meaning of this word. This is especially important at this point where we are discussing the correct form of Baptism, and the use of alternate, emergency forms, and how the Church views these various forms.

Baptism is a Greek word, and so we have to turn to the Greeks to find out what they meant by this word. As the saying goes, "The Greeks have a word for it." (Here, alas, the bitter truth must be confessed: sometimes, they don't have a word for it. For example, there is no Greek word for "toe." What we call "toes" are known in Greek as "the fingers of the foot," or maybe "little fingers." So if you look carefully [in a Greek lexicon], you will see that Greeks don't have toes.)

They did have a word for "baptism," however, and that word is baptisma; they had a verb too: *baptizein*—"to baptize." What did the ancient Greeks mean when they called something "baptized"? Hippocrates used the word, in its passive sense, to refer to something that was drenched. Eubulus the comedian used the word in reference to drunkards who were "soaked in wine." Plato used the term to describe debtors who were "over their head and ears in debt." And in regard to someone who was being interrogated, he used the same word to say "he was drowned with questions; he was getting into deep water." And finally, the historian Polybius refers to ships that were "baptized" during a sea battle, that is, they had sunk right down to the bottom of the sea.

At the risk of repeating a good story to an audience that may already have heard it, a few years ago a Roman Catholic priest came by our monastery, and I happened to be on telephone duty. During our conversation he asked, "Is it true that you Orthodox baptize by immersion?" I told him, "Well, you must know that 'baptism' is a Greek word that means 'immersion.' So what you're really asking me is if we immerse by immersion, and the answer to that is: "Yes!"

But why is immersion so important? Because it is a figure and symbol of Christ's death and burial. As we saw above from Saint Paul:

> Know ye not that as many of us as were baptized into Jesus Christ were baptized into His death? Therefore, we are buried with Him by baptism into death . . . For if we have been planted together in the likeness of His death, we shall be also in the likeness of His resurrection.
>
> Romans 6:3–5

In one of his homilies, Mar Jacob, Bishop of Serugh, who lived in the fifth and sixth centuries, brings out this link between our Saviour's death and the Mystery of Holy Baptism:

> Adam in turn slept, and his side was pierced;
> from it came forth Eve to be mother for the whole world,
> serving as an image of that sleep of death on the Cross
> and that side which gave birth to Baptism.
> Adam slept and gave the whole world a mother;
> the Saviour died, and there flows from Him baptismal water.[4]

Mar Jacob (among other Church writers) speaks of the water and blood that came forth from our Saviour's side on the Cross. The water is an image of the Mystery of Holy Baptism, the blood is an image of the Mystery of the Holy Eucharist. The one is the image of our death, the other of the source of our life.

In his beautiful homily on Moses' veil, Mar Jacob intertwines the themes of Baptism and death, of the Crucifixion and of Holy Communion, of the union of Christ the Bridegroom with His Bride the Church. In one remarkable passage he says:

> From the [baptismal] water comes the chaste and holy union
> of Bride and Bridegroom, united in spirit in Baptism.
> Women are not joined to their husbands in the same way

[4] Mar Jacob of Serugh, "On the Mysteries, Types, and Figures of Christ," trans. Sebastian Brock in "The Mysteries Hidden in the Side of Christ," *Sobornost* 7, no. 6 (1978), p. 464.

as the Church is joined with the Son of God.
What bridegroom died for his bride, apart from our Lord?
What bride sought out a slain man to be her husband?
Who, from the world's beginning, ever gave his blood
as the bride-price?
Apart from the Crucified one, who sealed the marriage
with His wounds?
Who has ever seen a corpse placed in the midst of
the wedding feast,
with the bride embracing it, waiting to be comforted by it?
At what wedding, apart from this, did they break
the body of the bridegroom for the guests in place
of other food?
Wives are separated from their husbands by death
but this Bride is joined to her Beloved by death!
He died on the Cross and gave His Body to the Bride
made glorious,
and she plucks and eats it every day at His table;
He opened up His side and mixed His cup with holy Blood,
He gave it her to drink that she might forget her many idols.
She was anointed with Him in the oil,[5] she put Him
on in the water, she consumed Him in the Bread,
She drank Him in the Wine, so that the world might
know that the two of them are one.
He died on the Cross, but she does not exchange Him
for another;
she is full of love for His death, knowing that from
it she has life.
Man and wife were the basis of this mystery,
they served as a picture and type and image for reality.
By means of them Moses uttered this great mystery,
covering up and preserving it under a veil so that it
should not be laid bare.
The great Apostle uncovered its beauty and showed it
to the world,
and so Moses' words 'the two shall be one', stood illumined.[6]

[5]Literally, "She anointed Him with oil," and translated thus by Sebastian Brock.
[6] Mar Jacob of Serugh, "Concerning the Veil on Moses' Face," trans. Sebastian Brock, *Sobornost* 3, no. 1 (1981), pp. 75–76.

And in his homilies on the Gospel of Saint John, our holy Father John Chrysostom elaborates the theme of Baptism and death:

> In Baptism are completed the articles of our covenant with God; burial and death, resurrection and life; and these take place all at once. For when we plunge our heads down in the water, the old man is buried in a tomb below, and wholly sunk for ever; then, as we raise them again, the new man rises in his place. As it is easy for us to dip and to lift our heads again, so it is easy for God to bury the old man, and to show forth the new. And this is done thrice, that you may learn that the power of the Father, and the Son, and the Holy Spirit fulfils all this. To show that what we say is no conjecture, hear Paul saying, "We were buried with Him by Baptism into death"; and again, "Our old man was crucified with Him"; and again, "We have been planted together in the likeness of His death." And not only is Baptism called a "cross," but the Cross is called Baptism. "With the Baptism," says Christ, "that I am baptized with, shall ye be baptized"; and "I have a Baptism to be baptized with, which ye know not." For as we easily dip and lift our heads again, so He also easily died and rose again when He willed; or rather, much more easily, though He tarried the three days for the dispensation of a certain mystery.[7]

In still another homily, Saint John Chrysostom notes that other people fish by pulling the fish out of the water, whereas we Christians fish by throwing the fish into the water![8]

> The complete immersion or submersion of an individual in Baptism is the figure of the death of the old man, and his emergence from the water as one reborn is a figure of renewal and the consecration of a new life in the figure of the Resurrection. We do not bury people by sprinkling a handful of earth over their heads or by shaking a little shovel full of dirt over them. No, we bury them completely, deep in the earth. Immersion, that is, Baptism, is one thing and sprinkling is another. They are not the same, and that is why the Holy Scriptures make a point of telling us that

---

[7] Saint John Chrysostom *On the Gospel of Saint John*, Homily Twenty-five.
[8] Saint John Chrysostom *On the Holy Pascha* (Migne, PG 50, 437).

Saint John the Forerunner was baptizing at Ænon near Salim, "because there was much water there." Indeed, why should Saint John the Baptist, or our Saviour, take the trouble to go all the way down to the Jordan River if any little washbasin elsewhere would have served the same purpose?

Assuredly, just as sprinkling a little earth over the head of a dead man does not count as burial, even so does sprinkling a little water over one's head not amount to Baptism, neither does it serve as a symbol of the death of our old self, nor even as a "likeness" of the death and burial of our Saviour.

Even elephants have more sense in this particular regard.

Have any of you ever been to an elephant funeral? Now, there's a funeral for you! Their time-honored observances in this matter are certainly most impressive. First of all, the prescribed form calls for a lot of mournful trumpeting and solemn stomping of the feet as the mourners circle the deceased. Then the bereaved elephants go off in different directions and break leafy branches off from the trees. They carry these back in their trunks and use them to bury the carcass of the newly-departed. Note that they don't just sprinkle a few leaves or throw a couple of roses over the body. No indeed. They completely bury it under the branches. So, in this particular case at least, even elephants have more sense than some people do. Instinctively, the wise elephant knows that when one is dead, one is dead and buried, not dead and sprinkled.

Returning to our own, too often less circumspect species, we observe that all the ancient authorities, including the Holy Scriptures, bear witness to the Orthodox tradition of immersion. The Jews themselves had their miq'uah, which was a ritualistic form of washing. Their "baptisteries," so to speak, where these rites were carried out, have been found throughout Judæa, and they are all deep enough to allow a person to be completely submerged. So deep are these fonts, that steps had to be provided, both leading in and leading out of these man-made pools. The very same is true of the ancient Christian baptisteries which exist to this day, for example, in Ravenna, Italy.

There can be no doubt, then, that for the Church in antiquity, and for the Church today, Baptism meant, and still means, complete immersion.

The Invocation of the Holy Trinity

Now we must ask what words are to be used when conducting Holy Baptism in its correct form. Again the Holy Scriptures and the ancient practice of the Church furnish the answer. Our Saviour commanded the Apostles:

> Go, therefore, and make disciples of all nations, baptizing them in the Name of the Father, and of the Son, and of the Holy Spirit, teaching them to observe all things whatsoever I have commanded you.
>
> Matt. 28:19–20

Saint Justin the Martyr, in his *First Apology*, makes reference not only to the invocation of the Holy Trinity, but also to the three-fold immersion, exactly as we correctly practice it in the Church today. And keep in mind that Saint Justin belonged to the first generation after the Apostolic era. If anyone did, he knew how the Apostles conducted Baptism. Here is what he says:

> Then they [the candidates for Baptism] are brought by us where there is water, and they are regenerated in the same manner in which we were ourselves reborn. For, in the Name of God, the Father and Lord of the universe, and of our Saviour Jesus Christ, and of the Holy Spirit, they receive the washing with water.[9]

And a little later in the same chapter, he writes:

> So that we should not remain children of necessity and ignorance, but of free choice and knowledge, and obtain remission of the sins we have already committed, there is named at the water, over him who has chosen to be born again and has repented of his sinful acts, the Name of God the Father and Master of all. . . . [Then] the one who is being illumined is also washed in the Name of Jesus Christ, who was crucified under Pontius

---

[9] Saint Justin Martyr *First Apology*, chapter 61.

Pilate, and also in the Name of the Holy Spirit, Who through the Prophets foretold everything about Jesus.[10]

The *Didache* likewise confirms this practice of immersion in the Name of the Holy Trinity. Another prominent text which affirms this usage is the early third-century work known as *The Apostolic Tradition*, ascribed by many to Saint Hippolytus of Rome, who is thought to have written it around the year 215. Here is the description of the baptismal rite found in this ancient document:

> After all these things have been done, let him [the candidate for baptism] be given over to the bishop or presbyter who will baptize. Let them stand naked in the water, a deacon going down with them likewise. When the one being baptized goes down into the water, the one baptizing him shall put his hand on him and speak thus: "Do you believe in God, the Father Almighty?" And he that is being baptized shall say: "I believe." Then, having his hand imposed upon the head of the one to be baptized, he shall baptize him once. And then he shall say: "Do you believe in Christ Jesus, the Son of God, Who was born of the Holy Spirit, of the Virgin Mary, and was crucified under Pontius Pilate and died and rose up again on the third day, alive from the dead, and ascended into Heaven and sat at the right hand of the Father, about to come to judge the living and dead?" [Notice how much this resembles the Nicene Creed, which was composed 110 years later at the First Ecumenical Council.] And when he says: "I believe," he is baptized again. And again he shall say: "Do you believe in the Holy Spirit and the holy Church and the resurrection of the flesh?" The one being baptized then says: "I believe." And so he is baptized a third time. And afterwards, when he has come out, he is anointed with the consecrated oil.[11]

In his *Mystagogical Catecheses*, which were written around the year 350, Saint Cyril of Jerusalem describes the same ceremony with these words:

> After these things, you were led by the hand to the holy pool of divine Baptism, as Christ was carried from the Cross to this

[10] Ibid.
[11] Saint Hippolytus of Rome *The Apostolic Tradition*, 21, 12–20.

sepulchre here before us. And each of you was asked if he believed in the Name of the Father, and of the Son, and of the Holy Spirit. And you confessed that saving confession, and descended three times into the water, and again ascended; and in this there was intimated by a symbol the three days of Christ's burial.[12]

In summing up this second part of our subject, I quote the learned Church scholar Fr. Georges Florovsky, who observes:

Holy Baptism, which according to the traditions of faith is performed in the Name of the One and Indivisible Trinity, brings salvation. The Mystery takes place in the Name of the Trinity, and [as Saint Athanasius the Great says in his Letter to Serapion,] "whoever takes anything away from the Trinity and is baptized in the Name of the Father alone, or in the Name of the Son without the Spirit, receives nothing. Those who are baptized in this way and those who think they are giving Baptism remain empty and unsatisfied."[13]

Then, paraphrasing Saint Athanasius, Fr. Georges continues:

In spite of the fact that the necessary words are spoken, Arian Baptism "in the Name of the Creator and His creation" "is only apparent and not real" because the words must be accompanied by true Faith. Baptism takes place in the Name of the Trinity because grace is received from the Trinity.[14]

These authoritative witnesses from antiquity establish beyond question what the Church's practice was and continues to be, both in the specific form that Baptism took (that is, immersion), and with what formula the Baptism was accomplished (that is, in the Name of the Father, and of the Son, and of the Holy Spirit).

The Correct Faith

Now we come to the third part of our discourse. We must consider,

[12] Saint Cyril of Jerusalem *Mystagogical Catecheses*, 2, 4.
[13] Father Georges Florovsky, *The Eastern Fathers of the Fourth Century* (Vaduz: Büchervertriebsanstalt, 1987), pp. 57–58.
[14] Ibid., p. 58.

though briefly by necessity, the doctrinal foundations of the Church's Baptism. Here we must ask whether the traditional, Orthodox Faith of the One, Holy, Catholic, and Apostolic Church is the only appropriate basis for a valid Baptism; or whether it is possible to have a valid Baptism established upon another, nominally Christian, credo? In other words, can Orthodoxy and heterodoxy equally, or even unequally, support the Mystery of spiritual rebirth, as our Saviour imparted it unto us?

Perhaps a little anecdote will help us keep on course.

Since our monastery—Holy Transfiguration—adheres to the traditional, ecclesiastical calendar and we have also been very vocal in our objections to Ecumenism, we are quite often visited by students, professors, clergymen, and once in a while, even bishops affiliated with Holy Cross, the nearby theological academy of the new calendar Greek Archdiocese in this country. These visits are often made with the purpose of trying to persuade us that the ecumenical path which their jurisdiction follows in no way compromises the Orthodox Faith. Virtually without exception, these good people open their defense with the words, "I believe," "I think," "I feel," or "In my opinion." But right at this point, we feel compelled to say, "Wait, wait! What you or I believe, or think, or feel, has no bearing on this matter. The only thing that is of any importance and has any authority in these matters is what the Church believes, thinks, and feels. If we start going on the basis of what each one of us thinks, believes, or feels, then we'll become like the Protestants, and in fact, soon we won't have just four or five hundred denominations as they do—we'll have millions. Each individual will become a church in himself, each one feeling, believing, and thinking as he sees fit. In this, as in every matter, it is the Church and its sacred tradition that must teach us, and we must listen humbly and be instructed."

What, then, does the Church say about the relationship between true and valid Baptism and the true Faith?

It is Saint Paul who provides the Church with Her battle-cry: "One Lord, one Faith, one Baptism" (Eph. 4:5). Not many lords, many faiths, many baptisms. Thus, from the very beginning, we are taught in unequivocal and unambiguous language that God, the Faith, and Baptism are inextricably bound together and are indeed one. There is no ecumenistic plurality here, no room for relativism.

Curiously, certain academic theologians of an ecumenistic turn of mind are not entirely happy with this "rigorous" interpretation of Saint Paul's dictum. They would say that this is the Cyprianic point of view. By "Cyprianic," they mean Saint Cyprian of Carthage, and by labelling this view "Cyprianic" they seek to create the impression that it was Saint Cyprian who was the "odd ball" who invented, or in any case vigorously promoted, this "hard line" view.

But is this true? Let us begin by taking a look at the Apostolic Canons. The Forty-sixth Apostolic Canon, in complete agreement with the Apostle Paul, says quite clearly, "We ordain that a bishop or a presbyter who has admitted the Baptism or Sacrifice of heretics be deposed. For what concord has Christ with Belial? Or what part has a believer with an unbeliever?"

Now, what shall we label this "viewpoint"? "Pre-Cyprianic Hard Line"? But there is more. The Forty-seventh Apostolic Canon says:

> Let a bishop or presbyter who shall baptize again one who has rightly received Baptism, or who shall not baptize one who has been polluted by the ungodly, be deposed, as despising the Cross and death of the Lord, and not making a distinction between the true priests and the false.[15]

And before any one makes any hasty statements about the Apostolic Canons, allow me to point out that they were ratified and accepted by the Ecumenical Councils.

Now, in the Sixty-first Chapter of his *First Apology*, Saint Justin the Martyr points out that those who do not assent to the doctrines of the Church, that is, those who are found in heterodoxy, have no part or portion in Baptism or the Eucharist.

And Saint Irenaeus of Lyons, who comes in the second generation after the Apostolic era, has this to say of the Holy Mysteries in his writing *Against Heresies*:

> So, where the gifts of the Lord are, there one ought to learn the

---

[15] *The Apostolic Canons*, Canon Forty-seven.

truth from those who have succession in the Church from the Apostles.[16]

Elsewhere in the same work, Saint Irenaeus speaks in even stronger terms about the succession of the Apostolic Faith through true bishops—who, in turn, are the ministers of the Holy Mysteries of the Church. He writes:

> We can enumerate the bishops who were appointed in Churches by the Apostles and their successors down to our time, none of whom taught and thought of anything like the mad ideas of the heretics.[17]

In short, as Saint Irenaeus points out, "the authentic Church has one and the same Faith everywhere in the world." "One Lord, one Faith, one Baptism." In *Against Heresies*, he states repeatedly that any false teaching regarding our Saviour or any corruption of the Apostolic tradition completely undermines God's redemptive work. Instead of building upon the rock of the Faith, which is single and steadfast, those who are in heresy build upon the sand, which—like their personal opinions and private interpretations—is multiple and constantly shifting.

The Church writer Tertullian was born around 155 A.D. and died around 240. Because of their genuine excellence, his writings, especially his early ones, are quoted considerably by later authors. He was also the first church writer to write in Latin, since Greek was beginning to pass away as a common language in the West. Later in his life, Tertullian fell into the Montanist heresy. But around the year 200, while he was still Orthodox, he wrote a book called *On Baptism*, where he describes in considerable detail the faith and practice of the Church. Here is the testimony of *On Baptism* regarding the Baptism of the Church and that of the heterodox:

> We have one and only one Baptism in accord with the Gospel of the Lord as well as with the letters of the Apostle, inasmuch as he says: "One God, and one Baptism, and one Church in the Heavens." The question, however, of what is to be observed in regard to the heretics may be worthwhile treating. The assertion

---

[16] Saint Irenaeus of Lyons *Against Heresies*, Book Four, 26:5.
[17] Ibid., Book Three, 3:1.

is made in our regard. Heretics, however, have no fellowship in our discipline. That they are outsiders is testified to by the very fact of their excommunication. I ought not recognize in their regard a precept binding upon me; for we and they have not one God nor one—that is the same—Christ. Therefore, neither is their Baptism one with ours, because it is not the same. Since they have it not rightly, doubtless they have it not at all; and what they do not have is not to be counted. Thus, they cannot receive the grace of Baptism, because they do not have it to give.[18]

Not only before Saint Cyprian, but also after him, the Church adhered tenaciously to this Apostolic teaching. In his work *On the Holy Spirit*, Saint Basil the Great speaks of the indissoluble bond linking the true Faith and valid Baptism. He writes:

From whence is it that we are Christians? Through our Faith, would be the universal answer. And in what way are we saved? Plainly because we were reborn through the grace given in our Baptism. How else could we be? And after recognizing that this salvation is established through the Father, and the Son, and the Holy Spirit, shall we fling away "that form of doctrine" (Rom. 6:17) which we received? Would it not rather be ground for great groaning if we are found now further off from our salvation "than when we first believed" (Rom. 13:11), and deny now what we then received? Whether a man departs from this life without Baptism, or receives a baptism that is lacking in some of the requirements of the tradition, his loss is equal.[19]

In his work *On the Holy Spirit*, Saint Gregory of Nyssa writes:

If, then, life comes in Baptism, and Baptism receives its completion in the Name of the Father, Son, and Spirit, what do the followers of the heretical Macedonius mean who account the Minister of life, the Holy Spirit, as nothing? ... What condemnation is thereby implied in those who thus defy the Holy Spirit? Perhaps this is the blasphemy against our Law-giver [the Holy Spirit] for which the judgement without remission has been decreed;

---

[18] Tertullian, *On Baptism*, chapter 15.
[19] Saint Basil the Great, *On the Holy Spirit*, 10:26.

since in Him the entire Being, Blessed and Divine, is insulted also.[20]

Saint Gregory explains that because of their erroneous belief concerning the Holy Spirit, the heretical Macedonians not only do not receive the grace of the Holy Spirit—in Baptism or in anything else—but they actually blaspheme against the Holy Spirit, and thus bring upon themselves a sin which is unforgivable.

The Sixty-eighth Apostolic Canon tells us the following:

> If any bishop, presbyter, or deacon shall receive from anyone a second ordination, let both the ordained and the ordainer be deposed, unless indeed it be proved that he had his ordination from heretics; for those who have been baptized or ordained by such persons cannot be either of the faithful or of the clergy.[21]

The First Canon of the Local Council of Carthage says that "those who are baptized by heretics shall be baptized again in order to be admitted to the Church." The Thirty-second Canon of the Local Council of Laodicaea points out that the blessings—which, of course, includes the sacraments—of those who teach false doctrines are, in actuality, maledictions that are inflicted on those who receive them.

Thus, it is clear from these holy canons that, since the "baptism" of the heterodox is not acceptable, the Church does not practice "re-baptism" when it baptizes those who come to her from other denominations.

All of the canons that I mentioned above were adopted and ratified by the Ecumenical Councils. These teachings, therefore, are not "Cyprianic." Rather, this is the Ecumenical and Universal Church speaking.

The Holy Councils — both Ecumenical and Local — also provided that in certain cases, by the application of economia, the external form of immersion, even if performed by a heretical clergyman, could be accepted, and the Church had the power to bestow grace upon this ritual, which, up to that point, had been no more than an empty social rite. But

---

[20] Saint Gregory of Nyssa, *On the Holy Spirit* (Migne PG 45, 1325, A, D).
[21] *The Apostolic Canons*, Canon Sixty-eight.

this acceptance had one very important condition: the individual so "immersed" had to ask to be admitted into the True Church. If he remained in his heresy, his heretical "baptism" remained null and void. Again, this viewpoint is not "Cyprianic." It is the ancient practice and belief of the entire Ecumenical Church.

In the year 314, the Council of Arles (in present-day France) expounded this teaching in slightly different terms; that is, it stated that the heretics do have a "baptism." The bishops who gathered in this council, however, affirmed that this "baptism" is of no avail to the heterodox so long as they remain in their heresy, and the false rite in fact works to their detriment. They must, therefore, join themselves to the Church in order to receive saving, baptismal grace. In other words, the hierarchs were saying that the heretical "baptism" was really an immersion that could be infused with the grace of Baptism, provided the heterodox involved joined themselves to the Church. Essentially, then, the position of these Western Fathers was identical with that of the Church in the East.

Whether the rite of immersion as practiced by the heterodox was accepted or rejected depended a great deal on whether their rites were identical to the Church's rite. Sozomenus, for example, records that Theophronius of Cappadocia and one Eutychius—both of them disciples of Eunomius the Arian—stopped "baptizing" their followers in the Name of the Holy Trinity, and began instead to "baptize" them in the name "of the death of Christ."[22] Hence, there was no way the Orthodox would accept even the external form of this so-called baptism. In fact, this innovation caused a stir even among the other Arian parties.

On the other hand, Saint Gregory of Tours in the sixth century records that Lanthechild, the sister-in-law of Saint Clotilde, Queen of France,

> was converted at the same time as her brother, Clovis. She had accepted the Arian heresy, but she later confessed the triune majesty of the Father, the Son, and the Holy Spirit, and received the holy Chrism.[23]

In both cases, those who were received into the Orthodox Catholic Faith were Arians, yet one was received by Baptism and the other by

[22] Sozomenus, *Ecclesiastical History*, Book Four, chapter 26.
[23] Saint Gregory of Tours, *History of the Franks*, Book Two, chapter 31.

Chrismation. In the first case, the Arians had changed the traditional rite; in the second, they preserved the traditional form. Today, except for the Monophysite Armenians, Ethiopians, and Copts, not one of the heterodox bodies preserves the Church's ancient form of Baptism This in itself is reason enough for the Orthodox to adhere to the Church's norm of receiving the heterodox by Baptism.

Ecumenism's position on this matter is radically different. According to this ideology, virtually everyone possesses valid baptism, provided "the baptisms are celebrated in the Name of the Holy Trinity and involve the use of water"—to quote the official periodical of the Greek Archdiocese in the Western Hemisphere.[24] However, as we have seen from the Church Fathers and Canons quoted above, this is not true; and yet this heresy is one of Ecumenism's basic tenets.

Some ecumenists apparently are confused and draw their erroneous conclusions in this matter from the fact that the Church does not always baptize those who leave a heresy and come into the Church. On occasion, as we have seen, the Church has received non-Orthodox by Chrismation, or even by the laying on of hands, or by confession. This, however, does not mean that the Church recognizes heterodox baptisms. It simply means that, on the condition of a non-Orthodox person asking to be received into the Church, the Church has the power and authority to grant grace and content to that which hitherto had had no salvific content. This was emphasized by the Sixty-first Canon of the Council of Carthage in 419 A.D., which noted that "the sacraments of those persevering in heresy shall obtain for them the heavy penalty of eternal damnation." So, in a twisted sense, the ecumenists are correct: as the Sixty-first Canon affirms, heretical baptisms are "valid" and effectual, not in saving those who receive them, but "in obtaining for them the heavy penalty of eternal damnation."

Who needs this kind of validity?

We see, then, that if the teaching which we have confirmed above by many patristic texts is "Cyprianic," then it is also Apostolic, Pauline, Justinic, Irenaean, Orthodox Tertullianic, Basilian, Gregorian, Local and Ecumenical Synodal, and so on. Very simply, it was and is the teaching of

[24] *Orthodox Observer* (30 June, 1982).

the Church from day one on down to our own times, despite contemporary private opinions to the contrary.

When I say "our own times" I am not exaggerating or just being rhetorical. Although our century has witnessed many academic, licensed "theologians" who have their own ideas about Orthodoxy, we also have a super-abundance of Saints who censure the former by the holiness of their lives, by their steadfastness in the truth, and by the supreme sacrifice which they made for our Saviour and His holy Church.

For example, we have the holy New-hieromartyr Victor, Bishop of Glazov, who died in exile in Siberia, probably in 1933.

Listen to this remarkable reply which the Saint made to the Soviet Patriarchate:

> I myself grew up among simple people, the son of a church reader, and I have spent my whole life among simple people, in monasteries. As the people believe, so do I believe, namely: We believe that we are saved in Christ Jesus by the Grace of God; this Grace of God is present only in the Orthodox Church and is given to us through the Holy Sacraments, and that the Church herself is the house of grace-given salvation from this life of perdition.[25]

In concluding this third and final portion of my talk, allow me—like Saint Victor of Glazov—to give you another Orthodox "grass-roots" view of heretical baptism. All this time, I have been quoting to you from Church Fathers, early Apologists, ancient documents from the second and third centuries, Local Councils, Ecumenical Councils, ecclesiastical writers, and academic theologians. But what about the "simple people" that Saint Victor speaks of? What about the ordinary lay people, the "Orthodox silent majority," the non-professionals, so to speak—what did they believe in this matter?

On December seventh, we celebrate the memory of a certain Orthodox woman of Rome. Her name is unknown to us, but we must surely call her blessed. In the year 474, the Arians raised up a terrible persecution against the Orthodox Catholic Christians. Sunilda, the wife of the

[25] *The Orthodox Word*, 1971, p. 118.

Arian ruler of Rome, took it upon herself to attempt to force one Orthodox woman to accept the baptism of the Arians. The woman would not consent, so the Arians seized her, took her by force to one of their churches, and immersed her into the water in the presence of the Arian bishop.

As she came out of the water, she turned to her handmaid who was holding a purse. She took two coins out of the purse, handed them to the Arian bishop, and said to him, "Thank you for the bath."

This so enraged the Arians, they dragged her out of their temple, tied her to a post, and burned her alive.

In her, truly, are fulfilled the words of King David the Prophet: "We went through fire and water, and Thou didst bring us out into refreshment" (Psalm 65:12).

By her intercessions, and of those of all the Saints, may we be counted worthy of the Heavenly Kingdom. Amen.

Note

Patristic texts cited above have been referenced by author and title and standard text divisions, since these works are available in several collections of translations, among them:

Roberts, Alexander, and Donaldson, James, eds. *The Ante-Nicene Fathers.* Grand Rapids: Wm. B. Eerdmans Publishing Company.

Schaff, Philip, ed. *A Select Library of the Nicene and Post-Nicene Fathers.* Grand Rapids: Wm. B. Eerdmans Publishing Company.

Quasten, Johannes, and Plumpe, Joseph C., eds. *Ancient Christian Writers.* New York: Newman Press.

Quasten, Johannes, ed. *Patrology.* Westminster, Maryland: The Newman Press.

Deferrai, Roy Joseph, ed. *The Fathers of the Church*. Washington: The Catholic University of America.

Recommended Reading

The Rudder, translated by D. Cummings. Chicago: The Orthodox Christian Educational Society, 1957.

On Baptism, by Tertullian.

Concerning the Baptism of Heretics, and *On the Unity of the Catholic Church*, by Saint Cyprian of Carthage.

Mystagogical Catecheses, by Saint Cyril of Jerusalem.

On Romans (Homily Eleven), by Saint John Chrysostom.

Hymns for the Feast of Epiphany, by Saint Ephraim the Syrian.

Saint Romanos the Melodos, "On Baptism." In *Kontakia of Romanos*, translated by Marjorie Carpenter, Vol. II. Columbia: University of Missouri Press, 1973.

Nicholas Cabasilas. *The Life in Christ* (Second Book, chapters 4–22). Translated by Carmino J. deCatanzaro. New York: St. Vladimir's Seminary Press, 1974.

Father Ephraim (now Metropolitan Ephraim of Boston) delivered this talk—here slightly edited—at the Tenth Orthodox Conference, held in Ipswich, Massachusetts, in June, 1988.

NEW AGE BISHOPS

We can enumerate the bishops who were appointed in Churches by the Apostles and their successors down to our time, none of whom taught and thought of anything like the mad ideas of these men who are propagating false beliefs.

(St. Irenaeus of Lyons, Against Heresies, Book 3, 3:1)

THE APOSTLE MOHAMMED

"What next?" You're almost afraid to ask, especially when you hear some of the things that are uttered by New Age, "Orthodox" bishops. You're afraid, because what you hear next may be even more distressing.

A case in point is the recent statement of Patriarch Parthenius of Alexandria, who declared:

> The prophet Mohammed is an apostle. He is a man of God, who worked for the Kingdom of God and created Islam, a religion to which belong one billion people.... Our God is the Father of all men, even of the Moslems and Buddhists. I believe that God loves the Moslems and the Buddhists.

> When I speak against Islam or Buddhism, then I am not found in agreement with God.... My God is the God of other men also. He is not only God for the Orthodox. This is my position.
>
> *(Orthodoxos Typos,* # 854, Athens, Greece)

The Greek-language periodical *Epignosis* (Dec. 1989. #20, Thessalonica), had the following commentary to make on Patriarch Parthenius' recent statement:

> So "Mohammed is an apostle" and the new-martyrs [who were slain because they would not accept Islam], then, are "not found in agreement with God."

> We also believe…that God is the Father of all men and that He loves both the Moslems and the Buddhists. God loves mankind, but He does not love falsehood and deception. He loves the Moslems and Buddhists, but He does not love Mohammedanism and Buddhism. All Christians do the same. They love the sinner but hate the sin. They love the heretics but hate the heresy. They love the deceived but hate the deception.

Epignosis then goes on to note that those who continue to commemorate Parthenius as an Orthodox Patriarch, "even though they themselves do not consciously serve the New Age," are "worthy of tears."

What is equally worthy of tears and a source of grief to Orthodox Christians is that this incident is not isolated. In fact, Patriarch Parthenius' statement appears to be part of a long-range program that is slowly unfolding before our eyes.

SYNCRETISTIC SALUTATIONS

Already, back in December of 1972, Ecumenical Patriarch Demetrius startled the Orthodox Christian world with his congratulatory message to Muslims on the occasion of their *Bairam* (i.e., one of two feasts that occur after the Islamic fast of Ramadan).

Demetrius' statement was reported in the newspaper *Orthodoxos Typos* (15 Dec., 1972) as follows:

On the occasion of the *Bairam*, Ecumenical Patriarch Demetrius addressed the Muslims throughout the world with the following words:

> "The one Great God of all—all we who worship and adore Him

are His children—desires us to be saved and to be brothers. Though we belong to different religions—and have nonetheless learned of and acknowledge the Holy God as the beginning and end of all things—He desires that we should love one another and think and do only that which is good in our dealings with one another. This is the present hour's commandment for the world: love and goodness. Of course, all faithful and good Muslims are filled with this same ideal, and with the same joy will accept this message of brotherhood in God, which is addressed to you on the great feast of Islam.

With congratulatory prayers, love and feelings of mutual goodwill of the faithful Christians,

✠ Demetrius of Constantinople

Alas, the truth is that "all faithful and good Muslims" are not, have not, and, if they observe the precepts of the Koran faithfully, probably never shall be filled with these same ideals.

HUMAN RIGHTS IN THE KORAN BELT

The usual Islamic attitude towards all others is demonstrated by the shocking incidents reported in the *Ecumenical Press Service* (Jan. 1–5, 1990). Although it is reported that these practices have stopped for now, the above-mentioned periodical noted that during the 1980's in Iran, Christians "were frequently exposed to attacks by the ayatollahs and mullahs while celebrating holy communion.... Christians were maltreated, communion cups were emptied and besmirched." The report goes on to say that Islamic revolutionary guards would enter Christian catechetical schools in order "to make sure that Jesus Christ was portrayed according to the Islamic faith, namely as a precursor of Mohammed and not as the Son of God. Those who violated this law were expelled from the country or hauled before an Islamic tribunal."

These incidents in Iran are not local quirks or deviations from the norm for Islamic governments, which are not particularly noted for their record on human rights. The Ottoman Turks, for example, were well-known—even throughout Moslem Arabic countries—for their inhuman ways. When they first overran Albania, the Ottoman Muslims cut out the tongues of tens of thousands of Christian parents so that the latter would not be able to teach the Christian Faith to their children. In Serbia, Bulgaria, and parts of Romania, entire villages of Christians — men, women, and children — were impaled on thousands of stakes planted along both sides of the roads. In Greece, similar massacres were frequent and were also accompanied by "the gathering of the children"—the abduction and forced conversion of thousands of Christian boys and girls. In this century, the genocide of the Armenian people by the Turks, overlooked by most of mankind, inspired Hitler and his Nazis to institute their extermination of the Jews and other peoples that didn't fit in their plans.

In our own days, the State Department's Human Rights Report for 1989 records that this litany of cruelty continues unabated in Islamic countries. The Report is quite harsh on the state of human rights in the "Koran belt." Both Egypt and Turkey are accused of torturing prisoners; in Turkey, the Report notes, the victims of torture have oftentimes been children. Libya is described as ignoring human rights altogether. In Syria such basics as the freedom of speech and assembly are unknown. Iraq and Iran have nothing but contempt for human rights. In Saudi Arabia there are no rights for women, no Christian churches are allowed, nor are Christian meetings permitted without special permission. The Koran itself is filled with exhortations to faithful Muslims to wage war against non-Muslims. Some samples:

> Fight those who believe not in God, nor the Last Day, nor hold that forbidden which hath been forbidden by God and His Apostle,[1] nor acknowledge the Religion of Truth, (even if they are) of the People of the Book[2] until they pay the Jizya[3] with willing submission, and feel themselves subdued.[4]
>
> (Sura 9:29)

> O ye who believe! Fight the Unbelievers who gird you about, and let them find firmness in you.
>
> (Sura 9:123)

[1] This is a Koranic reference to Mohammed.
[2] I.e., the Holy Bible.
[3] I.e., compensation.
[4] From *The Meaning of the Glorious Our 'an*, with a translation and commentary by Abdullsh Yusuf All, Cairo, 1934.

Therefore, when ye meet the Unbelievers (in fight), smite at their necks; at length, when ye have thoroughly subdued them, bind a bond firmly (on them).

(Sura 47:4)

And elsewhere, lest any conciliatory Muslims should "weaken" and display a reluctance for war and bloodshed, the second Sura of the Koran takes care to admonish and castigate them:

Fighting is prescribed for you, and ye dislike it. But it is possible that ye dislike a thing which is good for you, and that ye love a thing which is bad for you. But God knoweth and ye know not.

(Sura 2:216)

This warlike attitude is confirmed and encouraged even in contemporary Muslim writers. Here are some examples:

The Islamic religion is based on the pursuit of domination and power and strength and might.
(Muhammed al-Mutti Bakhit, *Haquiaat al-Islam*, Cairo, 1926)

The spread of Islam is military. There is a tendency to apologize for this and we should not. It is one of the injunctions of the Koran that you must fight for the spreading of Islam.
(Dr. Ali Issa Othman, quoted by Charis Waddy in *The Muslim Mind*, Longmans, London, 1976)

As author Issa Khalil (*Epiphany*, Vol. 10, No. 3) notes, "two prominent modern Muslim reformers in the latter part of the 19th and early 20th century, Jalalu-iddin al-Afghani and Muhammed Abduh, lamented the fact that the 'Islamic religion, which was founded on military victory and triumph, and which intends always to conquer new territories and achieve victory'" was in their time under the rule of foreigners. And Khalil goes on to note that these Muslim writers affirm that "anyone who reads but one chapter of the Koran would judge without the slightest doubt that Muslims are supposed to:

become the foremost warriors among the followers of all the other religions, perfect military science to the highest degree, invent the most destructive machines, and develop and broaden physics and chemistry.... Yet one cannot but be perplexed to find that (all this) ... was developed by the followers of the peaceful and peaceable religion, and not by the religion of war and conquest!

(*Al-Urwat al-Wuthga*, Beirut, Dar el-Kitab, 1970, p. 65).

In other words, the complaint of some modem Muslim leaders seems to be that their own followers were not the first to develop the atomic bomb! In any case, what happened to the ideals of love and goodness, with which—as Ecumenical Patriarch Demetrius assures us—all Muslims are filled?

NOT THE ONE GREAT GOD OF ALL

In view of these statements from the Koran and contemporary Muslim writers, Ecumenical Patriarch Demetrius' fraternal greetings to the Muslims seem more like efforts at appeasing a belligerent and brutal foe. However, what is more serious, his statement about "the one Great God of all," Whom we all—Muslims and Christians—"worship and adore," is simply untrue. The Muslims do not worship the one Great God of all: the Holy Trinity—Father, Son, and Holy Spirit. Only one with syncretistic or Masonic sentiments could make such a statement.

The Muslims themselves are quite emphatic that they do not worship the God Whom the Christians worship, and they are right. However, since Patriarch Parthenius went so far as to promote Mohammed to the rank of an "Apostle of God," we obtained a copy of the Koran to see what this new "Apostle" has to say about our Lord and Saviour Jesus Christ and the Holy Trinity. Here below, in parallel columns, we have given passages from the Koran and the Holy Scriptures so that our readers may compare the two and understand that, in truth, Christians and Muslims do not worship the same God.

The Koran	The New Testament

The similitude of Jesus before God is as that of Adam; He created him from dust, then said to him: "Be": And he was. (Sura 3:59)

In the beginning was the Word, and the Word was with God, and the Word was God. The same was in the beginning with God. All things were made by Him; and without Him was not anything made that was made.... And the Word became flesh, and dwelt among us, (and we beheld His glory, the glory as of the Only-begotten of the Father), full of grace and truth. (John 1:1–3, 14)

Christ Jesus the son of Mary was (no more than) an apostle of God. ... Say not "Trinity": desist: It will be better for you: For God is One God: Glory be to Him: (Far Exalted is He) above having a son... (Sura 4:173)

Whosoever believeth that Jesus is the Christ is born of God: and every one that loveth Him that begat loveth Him also that is begotten of Him.... For there are Three that bear witness in Heaven, the Father, the Word, and the Holy Spirit: and these Three are one. (I John 5:1, 7)

In blasphemy indeed are those that say that God is Christ the Son of Mary. (Sura 5:19)

Who is a liar but he that denieth that Jesus is the Christ? He is antichrist, that denieth the Father and the Son. Whosoever denieth the Son, the same hath not the Father. (I John 2:22–3)

They do blaspheme who say: "God is Christ the son of Mary... They do blaspheme who say: God is one of three in a Trinity: for there is no god except One God. If they desist not from their word (of blasphemy), verily a grievous penalty will befall

All power is given Me in Heaven and on earth. Go ye therefore, and teach all nations, baptizing them in the Name of the Father, and of the Son, and of the Holy Spirit: teaching them to observe all things whatsoever I have commanded you: and

the blasphemers among them
(Sura 5:75, 78)

lo, I am with you always, even unto the end of time. Amen.
(Matt. 28:18–20)

Christ the son of Mary was no more than an Apostle; many were the apostles that passed away before him. His mother was a woman of truth. They had both to eat their (daily) food. See how God doth make His Signs clear to them; yet see in what ways they are deluded away from the truth!
(Sura 5: 78)

Let this mind be in you, which was also in Christ Jesus: Who, being in the form of God, thought it not robbery to be equal with God.
(Phillipians 2:5–6)
But when the fulness of time was come, God sent forth His Son, born of a woman, born under the law, that He might redeem them that were under the law, that we might receive the adoption of sons.
(Galatians 4:4–5)

The Jews call 'Uzair a son of God, and the Christians call Christ the Son of God. That is a saying from their mouth; (in this) they but imitate what the Unbelievers of old used to say. God's curse be on them: how they are deluded away from the Truth! (Sura 9: 30)

Thou art the Christ, the Son of the living God. (John 6:69)
For the grace of God that bringeth salvation hath appeared to all men, teaching us that, by denying ungodliness and wordly lusts, we should live soberly, righteously, and godly, in this present age; looking for that blessed hope, and the glorious appearing of our great God and Saviour, Jesus Christ.
(Titus 2:11–13)

From the texts given above, anyone who has even elementary intelligence can see that the New Testament and the Koran cannot both be true and God-inspired. If one is, then the other is not, for they contradict each other on every important point. If Mohammed is an "apostle of God," as Patriarch Parthenius affirms, then Saint John the Evangelist, Saint Paul, Saint Matthew and all the others are not.

And this, precisely, is why countless thousands of New Martyrs were slain by the Muslims—because the New Martyrs, together with Saint John the Beloved Disciple, declared that whoever denies the Son, the same does not have the Father, and that whoever does deny the Father and the Son is of the spirit of antichrist.

Whom, then, are we to believe and follow? the Apostles and the New Martyrs, or Patriarch Parthenius? The New Martyrs, who were slain for their confession of the revealed Faith, or the Muslims, who, following the precepts of their Koran, engaged in this slaughter?

There are countless other anti-Christian verses in the Koran similar to those that we mentioned above. This, too, is why many were shocked when Metropolitan Pitirim of Volokolamsk, the head of the Publishing Department of the Moscow Patriarchate, declared on Soviet television:

> When I have my own printing-press, I will publish the Koran according to the most ancient manuscripts that belong to the disciples of the prophet Mohammed, and I will give it to Soviet Mohammedans.
> (*Vestnik Khristianskogo Informatsionnogo Tsentra*, #31, 26 Sept., 1989, pp. 2–3)

As one church writer remarked, "It is to be noted that the publication department of the Moscow Patriarchate has never published a single Orthodox catechism for wide distribution."

Korans for the Muslims, but no catechisms for Orthodox Christians...

In the meantime, Bangladesh has forbidden the importation of a New Testament translation in Bengali, the country's official language, because, say government officials there, the New Testament contains "objectionable statements." As the periodical One World (May, 1990) notes, "Some Islamic fundamentalist groups have apparently become alarmed at [the New Testament's] popularity among Bangladeshi Muslims," and thus, in contravention of the religious freedom guaranteed by the country's constitution, the Holy Scriptures have been banned there.

Yet, despite this open animosity that the Koran and contemporary Muslims display towards anything Christian, we now have Orthodox bishops who themselves want to disseminate anti-Christian and Islamic literature.

WE WAITED FOR MONTHS

In view of all these sorry developments, our article's title, "New Age Bishops," is neither far-fetched nor an exaggeration. Surely such a state of affairs is beyond heresy. It is, purely and simply, a complete indifference to what is true and what is false.

It is sad enough that Ecumenical Patriarch Demetrius, Patriarch Ignatius of Antioch, Archbishop George Khodr of Mt. Lebanon, Patriarch Parthenius of Alexandria, and Metropolitan Pitirim of Volokolamsk have all publicly expressed syncretistic sentiments about Mohammedanism; but what can one say about those bishops and priests who serve together with them as "concelebrants in Christ," or who commemorate them as "rightly dividing the word of truth"? Or what of those who continue to honor them as true bishops, and ask their blessing, and kiss their hand? Are they not, as the article in *Epignosis* says, "worthy of tears"?

Beloved readers, we waited several months before publishing this article in the *Witness*,[*] hoping that at least one bishop among those who belong to the so-called "official" Orthodox Churches would protest against these outrageous statements made by Patriarch Parthenius and the others. Unfortunately, not one has taken Patriarch Parthenius to task and called for a retraction on his part. By this, have they not proven conclusively that the only thing that is "official" about them is that they are full-fledged and official members of a syncretistic, world-religion organization — the World Council of Churches?

The only response was one made by Bishop Maximus of the Greek Archdiocese's Pittsburgh diocese in the newspaper *The Illuminator* (Jan.–Feb. 1990, p. 4). Bishop Maximus' article was well-written, although it was also somewhat incomplete and misleading. It is incomplete because Bishop Maximus went to great lengths not to mention Parthenius' name — the closest he comes to referring to Patriarch Parthenius is when he

[*] *The Orthodox Christian Witness*, Seattle, WA, v.23, #40, June 4/17, 1990.

writes that "the author . . . bears full responsibility" for what he said. With this we certainly agree. But what of those who continue to concelebrate with him and commemorate him as though he were an Orthodox Christian bishop?

In his response, Bishop Maximus also writes that "our Ecumenical Patriarchate and our Archdiocese, or any other Orthodox Christian who respects his (or her) name" do not believe in such things as "the author" teaches.

It would appear that Bishop Maximus is trying to say as discreetly as he can that Parthenius does not respect his name as an Orthodox Christian. With this also we must concur.

But what about Ecumenical Patriarch Demetrius, whom we quoted above, and what of Patriarch Ignatius of Antioch, and Archbishop George Khodr of Mt. Lebanon, who have made statements virtually identical to that of Patriarch Parthenius? And what can one say about Metropolitan Pitirim's promise to print the Koran and its anti-Christian exhortations? Do these hierarchs respect their names as Orthodox Christians? From what he writes, Bishop Maximus apparently feels that they do not. But then, how can they respect their names as Orthodox Christian bishops? Does Bishop Maximus continue to commemorate and concelebrate with these bishops (or with those who commemorate and concelebrate with them)—even though they have not retracted their statements, which were made publicly and openly? As an Orthodox hierarch, Bishop Maximus vowed at his consecration to uphold the holy canons and the Holy Tradition of the Church. With one accord, the holy canons and the Holy Tradition of the Church teach us to defend the Faith against those who pervert it and to break off communion with those who persist in doing so. Here, for example, is what the 15th Canon of the First and Second Council says specifically about this matter:

> As for those who on account of some heresy condemned by Holy Synods or Fathers sever themselves from communion with their president, that is, because he publicly preaches heresy and with bared head teaches it in the church, such persons as these not only are not subject to canonical penalty for walling themselves off from communion with the so-called bishop before synodi-

cal clarification, but they shall be deemed worthy of due honor among the Orthodox. *For not bishops, but false bishops and false teachers have they condemned, and they have not fragmented the Church's unity with schism, but from schisms and divisions have they earnestly sought to deliver the Church.*

This is neither "fanaticism," nor "exclusivism," nor "intolerance." It is simply the Holy Church's time-honored and Traditional (with a capital "T") manner of protecting its flock from the contagion and disease of heresy. Do loving and prudent parents allow their little ones to play with children that are sick with the measles, the flu, the Black Plague, or whatever? So also good and faithful shepherds of the Church do not allow the faithful to pray with clergymen or lay people who are diseased with the contagion of wrong belief.

In his article, Bishop Maximus goes on to say that if "there is some truth in other religions, this truth points to Christianity, as the true religion; it points to salvation in the Only Name under heaven in which salvation is given, the Name of Jesus the Saviour (see Matthew 1:21 and Acts 4:12)." In itself, what Bishop Maximus says here is true.

MOVING BEYOND CHRISTIANITY WITH THE WCC

Unfortunately, Bishop Maximus' response is also misleading, because, as it turns out, the Ecumenical Patriarchate and the Greek Archdiocese (to which he belongs) have very different views from those that he presents in reference to salvation "in the Only Name under heaven in which salvation is given." As we know, the Ecumenical Patriarchate and the Greek Archdiocese (as well as all the other jurisdictions of "World Orthodoxy") are all official and organic members of the World Council of Churches (WCC).

And what are the Orthodox in the WCC up to nowadays?

At an official meeting of a WCC committee that met in Barr, Switzerland, from January 9–15, 1990, some twenty-one Orthodox, Protestant and Roman Catholic representatives drafted a 2,500 word statement on

"Religious Plurality: Theological Perspectives and Affirmations." These twenty-one official representatives of their respective church groups cited the need for "a more adequate theology of religions" (it seems they feel that what the Church has taught for centuries about false belief and idolatry is not sufficient), and, in the section on Christology the participants affirmed

> "that in Jesus Christ, the incarnate Word, the entire human family has been united to God in an irrevocable bond and covenant. The saving presence of God's activity in all creation and human history comes to its focal point in the event of Christ." But, they add, "because we have seen and experienced goodness, truth and holiness among followers of other paths and ways than that of Jesus Christ...we find ourselves recognizing a need to move beyond a theology which confines salvation to the explicit personal commitment to Jesus Christ."
> *(Ecumenical Press Service*, 16–31, Jan., 1990)

Thus, Bishop Maximus' feelings notwithstanding (even though he too is heavily involved in ecumenism), his superiors—via their official representatives at the World Council of Churches—are "moving beyond" the theology expressed in Acts 4:10–12:

> Be it known unto you all, and to all the people of Israel, that by the Name of Jesus Christ of Nazareth, Whom ye crucified, Whom God raised from the dead, even by Him doth this man stand here before you whole. This is the Stone which was set at nought by you builders, which is become the head of the corner. Neither is there salvation in any other: for there is no other Name under heaven given among men, whereby we must be saved.

But while the Orthodox, Protestant, and Roman Catholic representatives were officially formulating their "theology of religions" for the WCC in Switzerland, other events were unfolding in the Soviet Union.

"OMMM, OMMM, OMMING WITH GORBY"

The above title given in quotes is the name of an article that appeared in *Mother Earth News* (March–April 1990). In this article, author Ben Finney describes an incident that took place at about the same time that the WCC representatives were meeting in Switzerland. Here is what he writes:

> During mid-January a most ecumenical group of spiritual leaders — ranging from severely garbed rabbis, long-bearded Russian Orthodox priests, and robed Hindu swamis to brilliantly plumed Native American shamans — together with parliamentarians from around the world and a collection of environmentally concerned scientists, met in Armand Hammer's conference center on the snowy banks of the Moscow River for the Global Forum on the Environment and the Survival and Development of Humanity.

> The forum itself constituted a kind of global consciousness raising—with environmentalists trying to get parliamentarians and spiritual leaders on their side for a worldwide campaign to save the earth, while the spiritual leaders were admonishing the scientists and technologists to mend their ways and to learn how to protect the environment. All of us looked forward to the concluding address, which, it was promised, would be delivered by President Gorbachev. So, at the end of the last session, the delegates were bused to the Kremlin, where, once inside the fortress walls, we were led into the old meeting room of the Supreme Soviet—the one you see in the old newsreels, where a huge statue of Lenin, standing with upraised arm and clenched fist, looms over the speakers.

> After an appropriate wait, first Gorbachev, then Foreign Minister Shevardnadze, entered the room and, as we stood to applaud, took their place on the speakers' platform. Times obviously had changed from the antireligion campaigns of Lenin and Stalin, for, along with Gorbachev, Shevardnadze, and academician Evgeuniij Velikhov, there sat on the speakers' platform

Bishop James Park Morton of New York and—resplendent in black robe, tall white hat, and full beard—Metropolitan Pitirim of Vlokolamsk. This juxtaposition of political, scientific, and religious leadership was calculated; in fact, the Global Forum was officially co-hosted by the Supreme Soviet, the Soviet Academy of Sciences, and the "Religious Communities of the Soviet Union."

But even though by then we were more or less prepared to see a Russian Orthodox priest in such a place of honor, we were not really ready for the spiritual invocation that opened the meeting. A frail Hindu swami, draped in an ochre robe and daubed with white body paint, mounted the rostrum and, after a few carefully reasoned and thought-provoking words, asked us to "repeat after me, three times: Ommm...ommm...ommm. No one was taken aback. In no time, this Gandhi-like figure had Gorbachev, Shevardnadze, and all the rest of us from around the globe ommming away in this citadel of failed materialism while Lenin, frozen in time, glowered in the background.

After a number of speeches, including a rousing call to action in the name of Allah by the chief mufti of Syria, Gorbachev had his turn and delivered a carefully crafted speech asking for the protection of the environment...

Incantations to Hindu deities... "What next?"*

A little while ago, one of our clergy was visited by a group of new calendar theological students who wanted to know why our diocese was not in communion with them and why we weren't members of the WCC.

---

* For our readers' information, here is what the *Random House Dictionary* (Second Edition, Unabridged) has to say about the swami's incantation:
Om (om), n. **Hinduism**. a mantric word thought to be a complete expression of Brahman and interpreted as having three sounds representing Brahma or creation, Vishnu or preservation, and Siva or destruction, or as consisting of the same three sounds, representing waking, dreams, and deep sleep, along with the following silence, which is fulfillment. Also **Aum.** [1780-90; >Skt]
In Hinduism, Brahma is the impersonal supreme being, the primal source and ultimate goal of all beings, and is the first member of the Hindu triad. Vishnu is the chief deity worshipped by the Vaishnava (a Hindu sect), and Siva (or Shiva) is the god of destruction and reproduction. It is customary to decorate Hindu temples with the "sacred syllable—Om.

Our clergyman replied that the reason we weren't in communion with them was because we didn't believe that their bishops were Orthodox. However, in view of recent developments, it appears we have to update our assessment. Now we are forced to ask: in what way are these particular bishops even nominally Christian? Can anyone answer that question for us, on the basis of biblical, apostolic, patristic, and canonical criteria?

WE KNOW THAT THE SON OF GOD IS COME

Since not one hierarch—not one—among the new calendarists and ecumenically-minded has called upon these New Age clerics to renounce their public displays of apostasy, and since all "official" Orthodox continue to commemorate and concelebrate with them (i.e., "business as usual"), then we must conclude that they are motivated by one of the following sentiments:

> 1) They don't agree with what their colleagues are doing, but they do not have the courage to do anything about it because they might lose their salaries and positions. OR:

> 2) They don't agree, but in a manner entirely consistent with a typically protestant and congregationalist (but not Orthodox Christian) outlook they reply, "What these bishops say is not my affair," or "That's just their personal opinion." Yet, Holy Tradition is very clear about how we must separate ourselves from bishops who teach error "with bared heads"; furthermore, Orthodox bishops cannot have "private opinions" which are in opposition to what the Church has always taught (and which, oddly enough, though "private," are proclaimed publicly over all the media). OR:

> 3) They are not concerned with what their colleagues and fellow bishops teach. OR:

> 4) They fully agree with what their colleagues teach.

What about the clergy and the faithful who belong to jurisdictions headed by New Age hierarchs? Among these, one will find those who don't agree with their bishops. But this is like saying, "I'm on this train, but I'm not going where the engine is going." The unfortunate fact is that by their membership, and participation, and financial and moral support of these modernist jurisdictions, they become equally responsible for all that their hierarchs say and do.

Of course, there are those who fully and whole-heartedly do agree with their pro-Islamic and syncretistic bishops.

And they, and the ones who say they don't agree, and the ones who show no concern, are all "moving beyond" Christianity, together with these individuals that are leading them.

In the face of such developments, the words of Saint John the Evangelist are especially timely and relevant for us:

> *We know that the Son of God is come, and hath given*
> *us understanding, so that we may know Him Who is*
> *true; and we are in Him Who is true, in His Son*
> *Jesus Christ. This is the true God, and life everlasting.*
> *Little children, keep yourselves from idols. Amen.*
>
> (I John 5:20–21)

AN ENCYCLICAL LETTER

of Their Eminences, Metropolitans Ephraim of Boston,

Makarios of Toronto,

and His Grace, Bishop Moses of Roslindale

CONCERNING THE THESSALONICA MEETING

In the Name of the Father, and of the Son, and of the Holy Spirit.
Amen.

SOME MAJOR DEVELOPMENTS have taken place recently in the
relations between fifteen Orthodox Churches and the World Council of
Churches (WCC), dearly beloved. At a meeting held in Thessalonica,
Greece, from April 29 to May 2, 1998, the representatives of fifteen Orthodox Churches (which are full, organic members of the WCC) recommended that the Orthodox take part in the upcoming WCC assembly
in Zimbabwe next December, but not participate in certain aspects of
the assembly, such as joint worship services and common prayers. The
Thessalonica communiqué cited also the use of "inclusive" language, the
presence of women priests and pastors in WCC worship services, the
discussion of issues such as homosexuality, and the WCC's tendencies
toward religious syncretism, as aspects of the WCC which the Orthodox
oppose.

John Newbury, a spokesman for the WCC, expressed doubts initially
as to how much the Thessalonica communiqué was in accord with the

instructions given to the delegates by their respective churches, but he acknowledged that this recent development will have "very far-reaching implications."

One press release emphasized that "the Thessalonica communiqué is highly critical of the arch-conservative factions within the Orthodox Churches, most notably in Russia, Serbia, Bulgaria and Georgia, who want all links cut with the ecumenical movement." According to the Rev. George Tsetsis, a representative of the Ecumenical Patriarch, the recent meeting "unanimously denounced those schismatic and extremist groups within the Orthodox Churches that are using the theme of Ecumenism to criticize the Orthodox leadership, and undermine its authority by deliberately misinforming the faithful, thus attempting to create divisions within the Orthodox Churches."

Ecumenistic churchmen often attempt, as in this instance, to "politicize" the discussion in these matters. Terms such as "arch-conservative," "extremist," "liberal," and "moderate" are employed gratuitously in labelling friend and foe, especially foe. But the One, Holy, Catholic, and Apostolic Church of Christ – that is, the Holy Orthodox Church – does not have "conservative" or "liberal" or "moderate" parties, nor does it have "high" or "low" churches, as the Episcopalians do. In Orthodoxy you are either Orthodox or you are something else. In the period of the Arian controversy, if one was off by one "iota," one was not an Orthodox Christian. There are oftentimes points that may be debatable, but even in these cases the sole authority that determines what is Orthodox is the Church's Holy Tradition, as embodied in the Holy Scriptures, the decisions of the Local, Ecumenical, and Pan-Orthodox Councils, and the writings of the Church Fathers.

Also, in the Orthodox Church, whether a person is a "schismatic" is determined by the holy canons, and not by those who are themselves guilty of repeated canonical and doctrinal transgressions, as the ecumenists are. Here is what The Rudder says about "schismatics":

Canon XV of the First-and-Second Council of Constantinople (A.D. 861)

The rules laid down with reference to Presbyters and Bishops and

Metropolitans are still more applicable to Patriarchs. So that in case any Presbyter or Bishop or Metropolitan dares to secede from communion with his own Patriarch and does not mention his name as is ordered and appointed in the divine Mystagogy, but before a synodical arraignment and [the Patriarch's] full condemnation, he creates a schism, the holy Council has decreed that this person be alienated from every priestly function, if only he be proven to have transgressed in this. These rules, therefore, have been sealed and ordered concerning those who on the pretext of some accusations against their own presidents stand apart, creating a schism, and severing the unity of the Church. But as for those who on account of some heresy condemned by Holy Councils or Fathers, sever themselves from communion with their president, that is, because he publicly preaches heresy and with bared head teaches it in the Church, such persons as these not only are not subject to canonical penalty for walling themselves off from communion with the so-called Bishop before synodal clarification, but [on the contrary] they shall be deemed worthy of due honor among the Orthodox. For not Bishops, but false bishops and false teachers have they condemned, and they have not fragmented the Church's unity with schism, but from schisms and divisions have they earnestly sought to deliver the Church.

The first heresy of the ecumenists – "condemned by Holy Councils and Fathers," and by the Holy Creed itself – is that the Ecumenical Patriarchate, right from the very inception of the Ecumenical Movement, in its Encyclical of 1920, recognized and addressed the various heterodox denominations as "Churches of Christ" and as "fellow heirs and partakers of the same promise of God in Jesus Christ." From this and from many subsequent developments in Ecumenism – as we have demonstrated on numerous occasions – it is clear that the title "schismatic" is directly applicable to the ecumenists themselves, since it was their own actions and decisions that brought about the schism.

The representative of the Ecumenical Patriarchate, the Rev. George Tsetsis, speaks of groups that are engaged in "deliberately misinforming the faithful," but he gives no indication or evidence of what this "misinformation" consists. On the other hand, countless photographs, videos, articles, pamphlets, and books have documented and recorded the un-Orthodox declarations and activities of those churchmen who are involved in Ecumenism. Their own signed statements with the Vatican and the Monophysites proclaim with bold eloquence their doctrinal deviations. Their own Patriarchs have set their signatures to some remarkably heterodox encyclicals and pronouncements. It is they, not others, who misrepresent Orthodox Christianity.

An open letter, written in 1995 by Archimandrite Nektarios Moulatsiotis to his new calendar hierarchy in Greece, is a fitting response to Fr. George's unsubstantiated accusation that some groups "deliberately misinform" the faithful. As Father Nektarios, a new calendar clergyman, notes:

> Unfortunately, we say one thing and do another. We are sometimes Orthodox in what we say, or sometimes unhealthy Orthodox in what we say, but we are certainly unhealthy ecumenists in our deeds. How is it possible for us to say that "Orthodoxy considers dogmatic unity a presupposition to the common Cup; for this reason we do not concelebrate with the non-Orthodox" (as Metropolitan Christodoulos stated on February 21, 1995,)* while [our encyclicals say] the exact opposite?

Also, how can we say such falsehoods when our Ecumenical Patriarchs have gone to the Vatican in an official capacity and prayed jointly with the Latins, and the Latins come to Orthodox churches and pray with Orthodox hierarchs? How is it possible to fool ourselves and others when we knowingly say these falsehoods? There exist an abundance of videos and photographs of such concelebrations and common Mysteries (weddings); is it possible to say that these things do not go on in Orthodoxy? Why do we deny the truth? Further, the distinguished Professor Evangelos [or, more likely, Andrew] Theodorou wrote an extensive article in *Orthodoxos Typos* last year and testified that, unfortunately, most of our Orthodox hierarchs are possessed by "unhealthy Ecumenism." Let us, at least, admit our tragic mistakes.

We all make mistakes, but here, for the purpose of this encyclical, we are discussing some very serious doctrinal errors made publicly and repeatedly by the ecumenistic "Orthodox." Let them, at least, admit their tragic mistakes. With this recent meeting in Thessalonica, they have taken a very positive step towards doing exactly this, and if they remain steadfast

---

*Recently elected Archbishop of Athens and All Greece.

in upholding their recommendations, they shall most certainly be counted worthy of praise and honor.

ONE DISTURBING ELEMENT about the communiqué from Thessalonica is the immoderate and misleading language ("schismatics and extremist groups," "arch-conservative factions," "deliberately misinform") that seems to betray anger or, at the very least, annoyance with those who are critical of these fifteen Churches' involvement with the WCC. The use of such uncharitable language against allegedly "schismatic and extremist" groups is odd--especially in view of the fact that the ecumenists are now recommending the very measures that the "schismatic and extremist" groups have said should have been taken years ago!

Are they upset because they are taking these needed steps reluctantly? Are they perturbed because the documentation, videos, and other information provided by the supposed "schismatics and extremists" have proven to be all too true, and that it has been demonstrated that it is actually they, the ecumenists, who are "deliberately misinforming" the faithful?

The case of the Georgian Patriarchate comes to mind. When this church withdrew (reluctantly) from the WCC in the Spring of 1997, it turned about and punished the clergy that had urged it to take this action! Obviously, the Georgian Patriarchal bishops then, perhaps like the representatives in Thessalonica now, were forced to take this step because so many of their faithful were protesting against involvement in the World Council of Churches. In the case of Catholicos-Patriarch Ilia II of Georgia, this involvement reached somewhat comic proportions. When he was elected one of the six presidents of the World Council of Churches in 1979 and served in that capacity until 1983, he proudly inserted his cherished new title into the text of his official commemoration during the church services: "For our Great Lord and Father, Catholicos-Patriarch of All Georgia, Archbishop of Mtskheta and Tbilisi, President of the World Council of Churches, Ilia II"! This single usage, however, did not suffice apparently, and so he began to use this newly-inflated title when issuing all his annual Paschal and Christmas encyclicals, as well as in all the published accounts of his ecumenical activities abroad (see, for example, the official publication of the Georgian Patriarchate, *Grapevine Cross*, No. 2, 1981, p.3).

PROBLEMS WITH THE WCC began to increase in 1991, when the WCC Canberra Assembly in February of that year included extensive pagan rites and presentations. The Orthodox delegates at the Assembly issued a Statement, expressing their profound concerns. Later, in May, 1991, at St. Bishoi's Monastery in Egypt, the Orthodox and Monophysite representatives to the WCC held a meeting in which they again expressed their anxieties, but also stated their view that, although there were disturbing developments within the WCC – for example, the animistic rites performed at Canberra, and other similar syncretistic manifestations – they felt, nonetheless, that it would be a "disservice" to Orthodoxy to leave the WCC. Regarding the Orthodox Church's membership in the WCC, they expressed the view that all the Orthodox Churches should either "leave together or remain together." A similar meeting took place in September, 1991 in Chambesy, Switzerland. After this initial flurry of protests, press releases, and soul-searching, silence descended like a curtain. Years passed, and nothing happened. It was back to business as usual.

Then, suddenly, in May of 1997, the Orthodox Church of Georgia, in response to sharp protests from its monasteries, convents, clergy, and faithful, withdrew – albeit reluctantly – from the WCC. This move sent a tremor throughout the "Orthodox" ecumenist world. Similar protests and calls for withdrawal from the WCC shook the Serbian Patriarchate in June of 1997. The WCC *ENI Bulletin* (Sept. 17, 1997) reported an interview with the Moscow Patriarchate's Metropolitan Kirill: "In reference to the withdrawal of the Georgian Orthodox Church from the WCC, Metropolitan Kirill told journalists that a small explosion in Georgia can become a tremendous explosion in Russia.'" Previews of that "explosion" were witnessed in the Trinity-Sergius Monastery outside of Moscow, on January 28, 1998, when a delegation headed by the WCC's General Secretary, Konrad Raiser, came face to face with the dim view that the Orthodox faithful have of the WCC's activities and its very reason for existence. The confrontation at St. Sergius' Monastery was not a happy one. Complaints were voiced that the ecumenist representatives – including bishops – were not truly witnessing to the Orthodox Faith, and that they represented only themselves and nobody else (nonetheless, they remain in charge of the ecumenist jurisdictions).

Alarmed and disquieted, the leaders of these jurisdictions saw that they were in real danger of losing the support of their clergy and faithful. Hence, the recent meeting in Thessalonica became an urgent – perhaps tactical – priority, in order to prevent further serious defections from their ranks. But even in Thessalonica, the representatives admitted that their resolutions were, as they said, "a compromise" to forestall further divisions among themselves. Nonetheless, the divisions have not been avoided, for at the end of May, 1998, the Patriarchate of Bulgaria announced that it too was considering leaving the WCC.

WE ARE ORTHODOX CHRISTIANS because we remain faithful to the written and oral traditions that we have been taught (II Thess. 2:15). These include the Holy Scriptures and the decisions of the Local, Ecumenical, and Pan-Orthodox Councils. It is impossible to deviate from or reject these traditions and claim to be Orthodox Catholic Christians. Ecumenist churchmen, however, have deviated from and rejected these traditions officially (as we have demonstrated in the past, and will gladly demonstrate again to anyone who asks us to do so).

Since this is the case, the recent recommendations made at the meeting in Thessalonica are good, but they need to be implemented and also supplemented by other courageous and steadfast steps that will bring these churches back into the fullness of the Orthodox Christian Faith. In ascending order of importance, these necessary steps are:

1) The new calendarists have to re-affirm and adhere once again to the decisions of the Pan-Orthodox Councils of Constantinople of 1583, 1587, and 1593 (we won't even mention the ten other local Synods that condemned the use of the new calendar).

2) Since Freemasonry is the matrix of ecumenism (and the religious syncretism which the recent Thessalonica meeting so rightly deplores), it too must be renounced officially.

3) Since Roman Catholicism has not retracted any of its errors, but has added other new doctrines, such as the doctrine of the Immaculate Conception ("a poor solution to a non-existent problem," as one Orthodox theologian observed) as well as the novel teaching of the infallibility of the pope, the anathema of 1054 needs to be definitively re-affirmed.

4) The jurisdictions of the fifteen Orthodox jurisdictions represented in the WCC – especially the Patriarchate of Antioch – must cease giving communion to those who do not accept and obey the decisions of all seven Ecumenical Councils.

5) The ecumenists need to reject officially their June, 1993 "Balamand Agreement" with the Vatican, just as a number of new calendar theologians and Athonite monks have already rejected it.

6) They need to disavow all those innovating hierarchs – both great and small, living and reposed – who led them into this pit of ecumenist quicksand.

7) And they will do themselves a great favor when they finally stop fooling themselves and abandon their membership in the WCC and all other related syncretistic organizations.

Most mainline Protestant denominations in the WCC are no longer interested in doctrinal orthodoxy. They, as well as hundreds and even thousands of Roman Catholic theologians and priests, no longer affirm such basic Christian doctrines as the virgin birth, deity, and physical resurrection of Christ.* They are interested primarily in "reshaping" Christianity. As the Rev. James Morton, head of the Interfaith Center of New York, said, "This is a reality sweeping the human family. The context has changed, people are now interested in a broader canvas." For these people, Orthodoxy is out, the New Age is in, with its all-embracing inclusiveness; no longer "in spirit and in truth," but in all sorts of spirits and relative "truths." The late Patriarch Parthenios of Alexandria (another President of the WCC) was very much in tune with the WCC's ideals when he declared, "When I speak against Islam and Buddhism, then I am not in agreement with God."

ECUMENISTS SEEM TO FEAR being "marginalized" if they drop their membership in the WCC. But "marginalized" from what? From denominations that adopt increasingly erroneous teachings? From offensive New Age feminists? From unrepentant gay activists? Why should the "world" and our neo-pagan society dictate the Church's agenda? The

---

* See, for example, *Newsweek*, August 8, 1993, Sister Churches--Five Hundred Years After Florence, Boston, 1994, and Christian News, May 18, 1998.

Church has its own agenda for the world. As far as the world is concerned, the Church is already "marginalized." In an article entitled "Pastoral Concerns" (*First Things*, Nov. 1997), author James Nuechterlein observes:

In the nineteenth century religious language and assumptions permeated American public discourse. Today they do not.

That is particularly the case in intellectual circles, and the clergy, like other educated groups, take their cultural signals from the academic and media elites. Informed by those elites of their marginal status – religion in elite realms is not so much repudiated as it is simply ignored – members of the clergy have flitted from one theologically tangential concern to another in search of cultural relevance.

The author cites a symposium on "Religion in America," published in 1968, which noted at that time "that religion is still worth talking about because it is playing a significant part in the social reform causes of the times: civil rights, peace, academic freedom, civil liberties, poverty, social justice in general." But now, in the nineties, writes Nuechterlein, "there are new enthusiasms." These include "sundry versions of feminism, multiculturalism, and ecological correctness." As a result, even "Orthodox" Patriarchs, worried lest they be left behind and become irrelevant, "marginalized," in the world's eyes, have hastened to jump on the ecological bandwagon. However, as Nuechterlein notes, "clergy anxious to recover lost [worldly] prestige" in our irreligious society "will not likely find it by invoking theologies of recycling" or concerns over pollution in the Black Sea. Judging from what we are taught in the Holy Scriptures and the Lives of the Saints, if Patriarchs – and all of us –were more concerned about being truly Orthodox and holy in God's eyes, our ecological problems would take care of themselves.

Let us bring to mind the words of our Saviour about how His followers would be "marginalized" by the world:

These things I command you, that ye love one another. If the world hate you, ye know that it hated Me before it hated you. If ye were of the world, the world would love its own: but because ye are not of the world, but I have chosen you out of the world, therefore the world hateth you.

Remember the word that I said unto you, The servant is not greater than his lord. If they have persecuted Me, they will also persecute you; if they have kept My saying, they will keep yours also. But all these things will they do unto you for My Name's sake, because they know not Him that sent Me. If I had not come and spoken unto them, they had not had sin: but now they have no excuse for their sin. (John 15: 17-22)

We Orthodox have more than enough of our own work to do without getting bogged down in the swamp of the WCC's inclusive agenda. We have spiritual, liturgical, and catechetical texts that need to be published for our faithful. We have missionary work that has to be done both at home and abroad. Our own people are in desperate need of patristic instruction. And we certainly need to get our own jurisdictional and administrative house in order.

The WCC has proven to be a doctrinal dead-end and, ultimately, a waste of our resources, and an occasion for sin. The representatives at Thessalonica have taken a praiseworthy step in recommending that their jurisdictions curtail their activities in that organization. May God grant them the courage to end this "tragic mistake" – their membership in the WCC – once and for all. And may our Saviour grant us all the fortitude to ever stand fast, together with all the Saints, in the good and holy confession of our blameless Orthodox Christian Faith. Amen.

Your faithful suppliants unto God,

✠ Ephraim,
Metropolitan of Boston

✠ Makarios,
Metropolitan of Toronto

Sunday of All Saints, 1998
Protocol Number 1502

✠ Moses,
Bishop of Roslindale